The
Goings

Praise for *It's Really All About God*

"Samir Selmanovic is asking the right questions at the right time, and refusing the consolations of certainty at a time when strident orthodoxies—atheist as well as religious—are perilously dividing us." —Karen Armstrong, author, *A History of God* and *The Great Transformation*

"This is an important book at an important moment in American history. As religious issues come to the fore internationally—and the influence of American religious leaders who preach 'my way or the highway' begins to fade—we need a new generation of believers who can articulate their own spiritual integrity while actively respecting the integrity of others. Samir Selmanovic is such a leader. Samir's personal and professional life has been richly formed by diversity. Now he offers us the fruits of his experience in this wonderfully readable book, grounded in his work in New York City with religious communities dedicated to honor and learn from 'the other.' We need a million more Samirs on the planet—people of conviction and humility who know that the vast mystery called God calls us not to the arrogance of 'ownership' but to the beloved community." —Parker J. Palmer, author, *A Hidden Wholeness, Let Your Life Speak*, and *The Courage to Teach*

"A remarkable book that combines memoir, insight, wisdom, passion, and compassion." —Marcus Borg, author, *Meeting Jesus Again for the First Time, The Heart of Christianity*, and *Jesus: Uncovering the Life, Teaching, and Relevance of a Religious Revolutionary*

"If atheists, agnostics, and nonreligious people like myself want to gain understanding and improve the world—not just complain about the evils of fundamentalism—we need to read not only the hard-line voices of ancient religions but also the freshest and wisest voices of modern progressive religion. Samir Selmanovic's is just such a fresh voice. I can disagree with him on theology—indeed, I can deny the very God he thinks it's all about—and yet I have learned much from his sensitivity, intellect, and generous spirit towards humanity." —Greg Epstein, humanist chaplain, Harvard University, and author, *Good Without God: What a Billion Nonreligious People Do Believe*

"Samir Selmanovic offers a deeply personal reflection on faith, doubt, and ultimately, spiritual peace. As the son of a Muslim father and Christian mother, Selmanovic was raised as a Muslim but later converted to Christianity, though his respect for Islam never abated. This unique interfaith background facilitates his telling a sophisticated and introspective story that simultaneously stirs the heart, challenges the intellect, and inspires the soul. Readers of this profoundly spiritual book will find themselves holders of a new and important perspective on their own religion, the religion of others, and even those without religion." —Daisy Khan, executive director, American Society for Muslim Advancement (ASMA)

"The author's spiritual journey has been truly unique. This puts him in a position to say some profoundly important things about God and the way religious people relate to God and to each other. You may not always like how the author says things, but he gives fresh meaning to the words of Jesus, 'Whoever loses his life for my sake will find it.' I *needed* to read this book and I am glad I did." —Jon Paulien, dean, School of Religion, Loma Linda University

"In a world in which religious traditions are too often digging in their heels into the tired sod of exclusionary self-righteousness, this love song to the God of all Existence is a much longed-for work of hope and optimism. Pastor Samir Selmanovic's expansive vision goes beyond polite formalities of 'interfaith dialogue' to urge us all toward new vistas of mutual learning, sharing and celebration of Life. Drawing from his own extraordinary life story—his conversion to Christianity and his growing discovery that both love and God thrive beyond its borders, he helps us celebrate the many miraculous and mysterious ways that the loving and life-giving power we call God moves through us all." —Rabbi Marcia Prager, author, *The Path of Blessing: Experiencing the Energy and Abundance of the Divine*

"I'm speechless in trying to describe this book. I laughed out loud in places and cried big tears at the end. It's a work of faith, a work of art, and to some, no doubt, it will be a work of damnable heresy. I think this book will change people's lives, and more: it can save lives, in the many senses of that word. All the religious pundits and broadcasters on radio and cable TV had better take notice, because this book threatens our conventional, comfortable categories and familiar black-and-white polarities. Selmanovic has the nerve to imagine our religions becoming not walls behind which we hide and over which we lob bombs of damnation, but bridges over which we travel to find God in the other." —Brian McLaren, author/activist (brianmclaren.net)

"For all Seekers of the Truth, Samir's deeply insightful, uniquely personal, lyrical quest for a relationship with God provides a clear vision of the need to dig deep, transcending traditional boundaries of faith and theology, be it Christian, Muslim, Jewish, Hindu. . . . —Rathi Raja, president, *Arsha Vedanta Center* of Long Island; executive director, Young Indian Culture Group

"Samir Selmanovic is a brave, compassionate, and wise spiritual teacher and community leader. This inspiring memoir/manifesto is a significant contribution to the growing body of literature on contemporary interreligious dialogue and action. Read it and be enriched!" —Rabbi Or Rose, director, Interfaith & Social Justice Initiatives, Hebrew College; coeditor, *Righteous Indignation: A Jewish Call for Justice*

"Samir has written a book that reads like an extended poem; an ode to life. Where others see only the darkness and destructiveness of religion, Samir sees beauty and hope. Where others see only competition and violence, Samir sees synergy and life. And his vision is no simple syncretism; a blending of all religions into one inoffensive 'smoothie' of goodness and light. This book is a celebration of postmodern 'otherness' of the first order. It will inspire you, frustrate you, maybe even anger you. Samir will not answer all your questions or tell you exactly what to do next. But if you've ever felt that nagging deep in your soul that God is lurking just beneath the surface in places you have least expected, you need to read this book!" —Ryan J. Bell, pastor, Hollywood Adventist Church (ryanjbell.net)

"This is a delightfully seductive book. In a conversational and imaginatively colorful style, Selmanovic leads the reader, gently but engagingly, along the steps of his own life's path to a conclusion that is as clear as it is challenging—that the only God worth believing in cannot be just 'my' or 'our' God. For all those committed to creating a truly multireligious civil society, this book is a gift." —Paul F. Knitter, Paul Tillich Professor of Theology, World Religions, and Culture, Union Theological Seminary, New York City, and author, *Without Buddha I Could Not Be a Christian*

"Samir has done what seems impossible—he's written a book about God that's fresh. Books about God, faith, and religion are a dime a dozen these days—but this one is so full of hope and enthusiasm. Completely honest. In the end, I found myself breathing more freely and wanting to love God and people more fully. I recommend this book!" —Carl Medearis, author, *Muslims, Christians, and Jesus*, and coauthor, *Tea with Hezbollah*

"Prepare to have your world expanded. Samir Selmanovic is like that voice in your head that causes you to reflect on the bigger questions. Jews, Christians, and Muslims alike will grow from this exploration of an un-managed God." —Rabbi Justus Baird, director, Multifaith Education, Auburn Seminary

"This is a solidly researched book that reads like a love song. My inner mystic jumped and leaped and shouted for joy. I found myself less lonely in this big old world. I felt like I was at a really good party, each paragraph a song, each page another glass of wine, each chapter the prospect of another dance with a beautiful woman. At this party, nobody got mad at me for letting my hair down. In fact, everyone, including God, encouraged me to go a little crazy." —Rev. Vince Anderson, bandleader, songwriter, honky-tonkist, co-pastor of Revolution Church NYC (reverendvince.com)

"In a most refreshing yet startling way, *It's Really All About God* confronts my Christian worldview and challenges my assumptions about God. But I understand that Selmanovic does not seek to persuade or convert, but to explore, to imagine with. His story is a remarkable demonstration of and testimony to the beauty and possibilities of radically God-oriented imagination." —Julius Nam, religion professor, Loma Linda University

"For those who love armchair travel, Samir Selmanovic provides a breathtaking report on his spiritual journey, one that has taken him deep into the thicket of interfaith encounter. This book allows you to experience that adventure through his eyes. It may move you to take the next step in your own exploring. If so, fasten your seat belt and bring Samir Selmanovic along as a guide. As more of us take those risks, I can't help thinking our world will be the better for it." —Rabbi Nancy Fuchs Kreimer, director, Department of Multifaith Studies, Reconstructionist Rabbinical College

"What if the excruciating tension between God and religion is not something to be denied but, rather, embraced as an act of loving devotion to both divinity and humanity? In *It's Really All About God*, Selmanovic offers a vision of spirituality that holds this tension as sacred. Rather than remain isolated in our 'God management systems' we can partner with each other across the boundaries that define us. The world would be better off and our religions would be more true, more just, and more beautiful." —Sammer Aboelela, community organizer, New York Community of Muslim Progressives

"This book nourished my soul; it fed my life; it centered me on what truly matters: life-giving, radical, and hospitable love. Samir Selmanovic has a way of telling stories that is simple yet profound, down to earth yet not bound, prophetic yet loving, and serious yet full of humor. I laughed, cried, and wondered. I became nostalgic for the home of my childhood and the 'thin places' where divine encounters occurred. Samir's love for life shines and his faith unsettles us. This is a powerful, moving, and empowering work, full of audacious hope." —Eleazar S. Fernandez, professor of constructive theology, United Theological Seminary of the Twin Cities

"Society is bearing a heavy cost due to our lack of meaningful discussion, growing divisiveness, and the mockery of religion. It is a long road back—or ahead—but Selmanovic has placed a roadmap before us. This book is epochal; it is for every atheist who is willing to converse and all the religionists willing to lift their head and look over the walls they have created." —William Bevington, professor of information design and former executive director, The Parsons Institute for Information Mapping, The New School, New York

"I am excited, unsettled, and inspired by the vision of It's Really All About God. Through sharing the story of his own faith and family, Samir shows how this growing vision of the kingdom of God has changed his world—and can change our world, too."—Nathan Brown, author, Nemesis Train

"Why are thousands not saying what this man is saying? Such obvious truth must be made even more obvious, and this is exactly what Samir Selmanovic is doing for all of us and for the future of humanity. After you read this wise book, you will say, 'Of course!' and 'Thank God!'" —Fr. Richard Rohr, O.F.M., Center for Action and Contemplation, Albuquerque, New Mexico

"In his book, It's Really All About God, Samir Selmanovic takes us on his personal spiritual journey, a journey that winds through different cultures, continents, and religions. The insights he gains along the way lead him to a unique understanding of the meaning of all religions, one that is grounded in the encounter with 'the other,' and one with which he intends to gently challenge all of us into rethinking what our faith means to us. Even if one does not agree with all of his conclusions, one can appreciate the invitation to go along on this journey as part of one's own journey to deeper religious—and interreligious—understanding." —Dr. Antonios Kireopoulos, senior program director for faith and order and interfaith relations of the National Council of Churches USA

"A keen and compelling storyteller, Samir Selmanovic has crafted a spiritual auto-biography that interweaves humor and lyricism with practical theology in a tale of conversion, embrace, and reconciliation. Provocative yet delightful, It's Really All About God is a welcome addition to the literature of interreligious relations." —Lucinda Mosher, Th.D., executive director, Religions for Peace—USA

"Samir Selmanovic delivers a message of vital importance to each of us in our increasingly interdependent world: that we only live the fullness of any of our religious (or nonreligious) traditions when we pay attention—serious, loving, and appreciative attention—to those outside our own faith. As a former Christian, this book filled my heart with genuine optimism that the vision of a human family, inclusive of and rich with all of our many different traditions, is not only necessary but also possible." —Phil Robinson, Leader, Joseph Campbell Foundation (JCF) Mythological RoundTable® group of New York

"How can our religions become interdependent, and thus viable and valuable, for the twenty-first century and our children's children? Samir Selmanovic has devoted his life to this question and *It's Really All About God* invites us to join him on the journey." —Bowie Snodgrass, director, Faith House Manhattan

"Anyone tired of the constant tensions between peoples in the world religions will enjoy this book." —Bruce L. Bauer, Chair, Department of World Mission, Andrews University

"This book comes at a critical time, offering help for those of us left wondering how to faithfully bring our traditional religious practice into the pluralistic world of the twenty-first century." —David Oakley, PhD, founder and chief science officer, WAVi Co.; founder, Addison College Project

"The Dalai Lama says that when he was young, he thought Tibetan Buddhism was the only way, but later came to know Christians, Muslims, and Jews, and realized they greatly enriched his life. He and Samir Selmanovic have a lot in common, as detailed in this fine, brave book, which explores, through personal experience, '. . . this treasure of difference, and why our first valid response . . . should be gratitude.' " —Marcia Kelly, author, *Sanctuaries* and *100 Graces*

Samir Selmanovic

IT'S REALLY ALL ABOUT

GOD

How

ISLAM, ATHEISM,
AND JUDAISM MADE ME
A BETTER CHRISTIAN

JOSSEY-BASS
A Wiley Imprint
www.josseybass.com

Published by Jossey-Bass
A Wiley Imprint
989 Market Street, San Francisco, CA 94103-1741—www.josseybass.com

Photo credit p. 171, Cathy McIntosh. Photo credits pp. xiii, 21, 45, 65, 95, 151, 225, 251, Joanne Clapp
Fullagar.

Permissions appear in the Notes section pp. 287-292. This is a continuation of the copyright page.

Readers should be aware that Internet Web sites offered as citations and/or sources for further
information may have changed or disappeared between the time this was written and when it is read.

Limit of Liability/Disclaimer of Warranty: While the publisher and author have used their best efforts
in preparing this book, they make no representations or warranties with respect to the accuracy or
completeness of the contents of this book and specifically disclaim any implied warranties of
merchantability or fitness for a particular purpose. No warranty may be created or extended by sales
representatives or written sales materials. The advice and strategies contained herein may not be
suitable for your situation. You should consult with a professional where appropriate. Neither the
publisher nor author shall be liable for any loss of profit or any other commercial damages, including
but not limited to special, incidental, consequential, or other damages.

Jossey-Bass books and products are available through most bookstores. To contact Jossey-Bass directly
call our Customer Care Department within the U.S. at 800-956-7739, outside the U.S. at 317-572-3986,
or fax 317-572-4002.

Jossey-Bass also publishes its books in a variety of electronic formats. Some content that appears in
print may not be available in electronic books.

Originally published as *It's Really All About God: Reflections of a Muslim Atheist Jewish Christian*

Library of Congress Cataloging-in-Publication Data

Selmanovic, Samir, date.
  It's really all about God : How Islam, atheism, and Judaism made me a better Christian
Samir Selmanovic.–1st ed.
    p. cm.
  Includes bibliographical references and index.
  ISBN 978-0-470-43326-3 (cloth)
  ISBN 978-0-470-92341-2 (alk. paper); 978-0-470-52729-0 (ebk); 978-0-470-52730-6 (ebk);
   978-0-470-52731-3 (ebk);
  1. God (Christianity) 2. Christianity and other religions. 3. Christianity and atheism. 4. Abrahamic
religions. I. Title.
  BT103.S42 2009
  261.2–dc22

                                                                                      2009021548

Printed in the United States of America

FIRST EDITION

HB Printing   10 9 8 7 6 5 4 3 2 1
PB Printing   10 9 8 7 6 5 4 3 2 1

CONTENTS

Dedicated to four Gospels:

Roy Naden

Rafael Candelaria

Rod Colburn

and

Brian McLaren.

You have been saving my life.

ACKNOWLEDGMENTS

Thank you, my mom, Marta; my dad, Sead; and my sister, Bisera, for teaching me how to live and love well. Thank you, Vesna, Ena, and Leta, my dearest. We did it!

Thank you, *everyone* from Citylights, Faith House Manhattan, and other beloved communities that sustain my life.

My gratitude to everyone mentioned in this book and all of you who have been throwing logs on my fire, comforting me when bruised, and helping me cope with this difficult and beautiful space of diversity, especially Bill Ashlock, Ryan Bell, Nathan Brown, Norm Buggel, Russell Chin, Lynette Darken, Robert Darken, Jennifer Elwood, Sean Evans, Ted Ewing, Lawrence Geraty, Dragutin Matak, Julius Nam, Jon Paulien, Alvin Poblacion, Rosemary Poblacion, Monte Sahlin, Helme Silvet, Mary Yeager, and Zane Yi.

Thank you, everyone who has gardened this manuscript with me, particularly my mentor and friend, master gardener in his own right, Professor Roy Naden, who has generously poured himself out in every season. Your kindness, patience, and skill kept me whole. My gratitude to my wonderful literary agent, Greg Daniel; to an extraordinary editor and human being, Sheryl Fullerton, a good fairy that every writer dreams of, and the entire team at Jossey-Bass/Wiley. And to those of you who have gifted a part of yourself to both the writer and the writing: Sammer Aboelela, Horace Alexander, Chad Allen, Vince Anderson, Justus Baird, William Bevington, Melvin Bray, Mari Brown, Todd Chobotar, Eleazar Fernandez, Nancy Fuchs-Kreimer, Fritz Guy, Marcia Kannry, Justin Kim, Paul Knitter, James Mills, Lucinda Mosher, David Oakley, Marcia Prager, Rathi Raja, Phil Robinson, Robin Simmons, and Bowie Snodgrass.

I am grateful to those of you whose influence, professional help, friendship, and support sustained me while writing this book: Nurah Amatullah, Christina and Raj Attiken, Jay Bakker, Lauralea Banks, Iowaka Barber, Ken and Diana Bauer, Erich Baumgartner, Jessica Binkley, Paulina and Rajko Biševac, Laura Bothwell, Troy Bronsink, Mary-Ann Broussat, Ruth Broyde Sharone, Elyse Bryant, Toan Bui, Tony Campolo, Osman and Ervin Čengić, Robert Chase, Yo Colburn, Eunice Cordoba, David Crumm, Bonnie Dwyer, Jon Dybdahl, Greg Epstein, Marry Erra, Jackie Evans, Fred and Anabel Facemire, Jim and Janelle Fazio, Duane Fike, Sieghard Frischmann, Lynne Fujimoto, Eric Gang, Jeff Gang, Becky Garrison, Juliet Rabia Gentile, Christine and Tim Gilman, Kim and Shelby Goerlitz, Sheila

Gordon, Marc Greenberg, Lisa Sharon Harper, Christina Harris, Steve Hatzman, Peter Heltzel, Sylvia Hordosch, David Ingber, Amanda Jackson, Kurt and Michelle Johns, Greg and Darla Johnson, Ryan Jones, Tony Jones, Kevin and Michelle Kaiser, Daisy Khan, Michael Knecht, Julijana and Milorad Kojić, Cheryl Lake, Amichai Lau-Lavie, Ronald Lawson, Samuel Leonor, Dragutin Lipohar, Greg Loewen, Sam and Sarah McCash, John Khabir McGeehan, Mitch McKee, Jill Minkoff, Josip Moćnik, Ector and Audrey Mojica, Titus Müller, David Oceguera, Andy Padre, Doug Pagitt, Eboo Patel, Victor and Denorah Pechaty, Dunja Pechstein, Stephen Phelps, Jan Podsednik, Luiza Purice, Nancy Raquet, Heather Reifsnyder, Paul Richardson, Tony Romeo, Or Rose, Desire Santos-Kho, Maria Sargent-Wayne, Frieder Schmid, Greg and Mary Schramer, Lorie Suntree, Larry Thomas, Miroslav Volf, Jerald Whitehouse, Darlene Zaft, and Jennifer Zosa. May your kindness keep on watering the world.

This book belongs to you my family, friends, neighbors, colleagues, and a multitude of other people that my life depends on. I don't know where my words stop and yours begin.

Samir Selmanovic

INTRODUCTION

The credits of the movie *An Inconvenient Truth* were still rolling when my wife, Vesna, and I sprang up from our sofa to tidy our apartment and move on with our lives. But our daughters, Leta (eleven) and Ena (thirteen) went silently to their room, so I followed to tuck them into bed.

"What is it?" I asked them as they looked up at me from their pillows.

"What have you done?" Leta said, without a trace of a smile.

I just stood there.

We just stood there. You and I.

Our children are looking at us, holding their breath in silence. Their unspoken accusations and mute hopes are not only about the physical environment of the world we are leaving for them; they are also about the spiritual environment they are inheriting.

I have been in the "religion business" for twenty years now, and this book is my way to enter this silence, grieve, ask for forgiveness, and look for signs of new life. Our religions—by which I mean any *systems of meaning*—are the caretakers of the spiritual environment of the world. What have we done?

We have come to the place where millions of people say, "Religion? No thanks. I'd rather be spiritual than religious." But our departure from religion is at the very same time a departure from its rich treasures of community, insight, art, practice, organized action, and hard lessons. Without religion, we find ourselves isolated, incoherent, and naïve on our spiritual journeys.

As Phyllis Tickle, author of *The Divine Hours* and *The Great Emergence*, observed in an e-mail, "All faiths are alike in their wisdom, more or less. It's in our mysteries where we differ." An honest conversation about our religions is, therefore, an intimate endeavor. Only when we believe that *the other* is not there to hurt us—though the other may struggle to understand us—can we begin to share not only the light but also the shadows of our religion. To step into such conversations, we have to be ready to embrace the holy awkwardness that surrounds our God talk.

Life is so wide and so deep that our religions are barely adequate to help us take it in. *It's Really All About God* is another way to say *It's Really Not All About Religion*. This book is an attempt to step above, under, or sideways from our religions and look at them not merely as their adherents but as human beings. I wrote this book because I believe that love for our religion is meant to be as dynamic as any love relationship. There must be a distance and not only an embrace—a tension. *It's Really All About God* is an invitation to acknowledge that distance and find a safe, honest, and hopeful relational place where wholesome love for our religions can thrive.

Religion, held properly, can change, and that gives me hope as we face our children. Religions are living things, and our children and our children's children need to see us treating religions as such.

Some of my Muslim, atheist, Jewish, and Christian friends understand the subtitle of this book—*Reflections of a Muslim Atheist Jewish Christian*—as describing a person who embraces four religious traditions at once. I am not sure such a person exists. But the concept makes sense to them nevertheless. "Hyphenated belonging" is becoming a reality for many people who have found truth, beauty, and justice—in other words, life—in more than one Scripture, tradition, or practice. In their experience, being asked to make up their mind and renounce one religion in order to embrace another would be akin to being forced to choose one parent and deny the other or to rely on one sense at the expense of the others. The way religions contradict or collide with one another is not nearly as important to them as the way they complement and illuminate one another.

In the interest of full disclosure, I must confess that the mystery that upholds my life is informed by Christian texts, history, and community. The cradle of my religious faith is Protestantism of a rather evangelical sort. For me, the subtitle of this book is a string of adjectives modifying the noun *Christian*. I embrace all the honor and shame that come with this identity. Yet I am not *merely* Christian. There is no such thing. None of us is a clone produced by our religion, not even people who try very hard to be one.

The other—individuals or groups that are not like us—is always there, affecting us, hurting us, blessing us, changing us. And because of this, we are all irrevocably unique. I would not have become or stayed Christian without the blessings of Islam, atheism, and Judaism. My hope is that Muslims, atheists, Jews, and Christians who read this book will hear one more voice affirming how indispensable our differing treasures are—and not just for ourselves, but for others, too. To maintain the breath of life in something as complex and beautiful as human experience, our mysteries need one another.

This book is mostly about four systems of meaning—the three Abrahamic faiths and atheism. As much as I had wanted to expand the pegs of the tent of this book, I soon realized that I cannot do everything at once. I am neither qualified nor capable. I do expect, though, that the treasures of other religions will reveal themselves between the lines in every chapter of this book and bless us more and more as our conversation deepens and expands.

This is not a book about Christian pluralism, so for those of you who are interested in my views on this matter, I direct you to a splendid article written by a friend who is one of my mentors, Professor Paul Knitter, "My God Is Bigger than Your God,"[1] as well as chapters I have contributed to two other books.[2]

Many questions raised in this book have been asked before. But questions that matter sooner or later reappear among us in new forms and with increased stakes. To address them, I do not offer a systematic interdisciplinary research work. Many fine books of that sort have already been written. Instead, I offer my personal stories and reflections, adding one voice to many others reporting from their life experience, the ultimate lab of all research.

Our Scriptures have spoken to us, and our lives ought to speak back. That's how we love our religions, challenge them, care for them, transform them, and help them deliver their promises to the world.

Our children are gazing at us, hoping in us. Theirs is the gaze of God.

To enhance your reading experience and help include more voices in our conversation, I suggest the following:

1. Organize a book discussion group using the Reader's Guide in the back of the book.

2. Visit the Web site http://www.itsreallyallaboutgod.com for additional information, podcasts, ideas, events, and links to social networking sites.

3. Write an *It's Really All About God* book review for Amazon .com, Barnesandnoble.com, Borders.com, or a blog. Your experiences and candid comments will help others.

4. Suggest *It's Really All About God* to a friend, colleague, book club, blogger, religious community, civic group, college class, or any group interested in diversity, cooperation, religion, spirituality, secular space, or interfaith issues. Together organize an event in your community. Serve together. Celebrate the gift of life together.

PROLOGUE

LIFE WINS

On a cold Saturday morning in December 2001, Soo Lee waited for her already-late friend on a busy street corner in Manhattan. She discovered she was standing in front of the doors of an old limestone church off Park Avenue where I was the pastor. Its large red doors were symbols of the large hands of God embracing everyone who ventured inside. That's what God was all about, I thought—inviting people in.

> *That's what God was all about, I thought—inviting people in.*

For Soo and most of her friends, church was a treacherous place. But the cold was biting, and the doors were unlocked. It was Christmas, and I had titled my sermon "The Magic of Christianity." Soo was a lively and tender young Korean woman who followed the spiritual path of White Magic and the Wicca religion, and the words "magic" and "Christianity" together drew her from the foyer into the sanctuary. She sat and listened to a story about a stable in Bethlehem, a magical moment in human history when, as Christians believe, the physical world as it appears to us humans and the spiritual world of God's Kingdom—the world as it really is—interpenetrated and became one.

Soo, as I later learned, is a person of uncommon stamina, a single mom, an urbanite who had learned to handle the grind of New York City with the smile of a marathon runner who has found a groove in the midst of pain. My wife and I loved spending time with her. We liked the way she thoughtfully constructed her sentences. We liked the way she paid attention to what we didn't say as much as to what we said. And we liked the way she treated everyone and everything around her. With compassion. Over the next several months, Soo and her little son, Tristan, became family friends. Soon we were caring for her boy and she was caring for our little daughters.

Some months after we met Soo, my church hosted the annual gathering of a national network I belonged to that consisted of mostly professional clergy and church leaders. The main service was going to include a closing segment we titled "Testimonies of Failure," with six leaders who would tell us how they had failed in their religious work. It was not to be "how God turned things around for me" or "how my failure has actually been a blessing." There would be no explanations, no justifications—just standing up, sharing the misery, and sitting down. I had a month to find someone who could address these hurting people with some healing words.

I thought of people who had cared for and encouraged me, and Soo immediately came to mind. But the thought seemed preposterous. Soo? How could I ask a witch to pray over a group of pastors? She could neither defend nor advocate for our religion—she was an outsider. But the experience of being a part of Soo's life had opened a crack in the wall that separates "us" (those on the inside) from "them" (those on the outside). Then a thought broke through, a possibility that I found both burdensome and exhilarating. What if God is on the outside too? Does God have to be absent out there in order to be present in here?

The thought of inviting Soo into the inner sanctum of our Christian experience ripened like wine, intoxicating my orthodox faith. Everything I had been taught told me that God, in God's infinite wisdom and love, has chosen to dwell in *our religion*. It was a kind of certainty one can stake one's life on. But then everything I had experienced with Soo—and, as I began recalling, others like her over the years—told me that God dwells in the *lives of people*. All people. Drunk with these thoughts, I hesitated. Which should win? Religion? Or life? Should I use life to prop up my religion? Or should I use my religion to honor life?

"Okay, I'll do it," Soo said with a smile when I asked her. Then she added, "But only if I can pray to God as Mother."

"Soo," I said, and paused, taking time to swallow a momentary feeling of regret for approaching her at all, "some of these religious leaders are worn out and beaten down, and on that day, our goal is not to expand their theology but to comfort them."

"I understand, Pastor Samir. That's all right. For now. Let's leave the discussion about the Christian obsession with phallic power for some other time," she said with a gracious smile. "Is it okay if I pray to God as Holy Spirit?"

"Wonderful," I said, relieved.

On the day of the gathering, after the six "losers" had shared their stories, the congregation was quiet, stunned by tales of the stark reality behind much of religious work and community organizing. Most of us religious people who go to our places of worship to receive religious goods and services assume that our faith is triumphantly marching forward on all fronts. Nobody wants to be a part of a losing battle. So talking about failures devoid of happy endings created an unbearably empty space in our hearts.

The sacred Scriptures say that in emptiness, God creates.

Then it was Soo's turn to pray. After introducing her to the crowd, I stepped aside, regretting my choice again, my jaws tightening, my palms sweating. How did I get myself into a situation of bringing a witch to bless a conservative Christian crowd? Did I want to lose my job?

Or was I heeding the call of Jesus—losing my life in order to find it?

With the steady voice of a person who has no doubts that our ordinary lives are saturated with the Presence, she said, "Dear

Holy Spirit, I am not a Christian. But I and my son are cared for in this church. These people who follow you work very hard to make a difference in the world and love people like us. Now they are tired, disoriented, discouraged. Please, make them see how important their work really is. What would our world be without people like them? Help them continue caring so that people like me might find a better way."

There are religious experiences that have the power to restart our hearts, when fresh faith in God, humanity, and world is uploaded into our soul systems. This was one of those moments. A hush fell over the crowd, and Soo's words lingered in the air like a sweet heathen scent. While some sat there paralyzed by the offense of her presence at the church pulpit, many of us basked in her compassion for us. We were hoping that if we just stayed quiet, there would be more words from her, interceding to our God on our behalf.

Life won.

After the crowd dispersed, I sat on a pew in the empty sanctuary to jot down these words in my notebook: "We are scared of finding our God *in the other*. Why do we fear something so wonderful?"

UNBEARABLE CERTAINTY

At different times in my life, I have belonged to Muslim, atheist, and Christian camps. In every one, I was rather certain. I believed that we—whichever "we" I was a part of—were right. And for us to be right, I thought, others had to be wrong. There were insiders and there were outsiders, and I found comfort in being on the inside.

Even now, in my early forties, I know I cannot survive without *some* kind of certainty. To live, I need some stable ground to live on, a soil from which I can sustain my life, a place where I can pitch my tent, a landing where I can make friends.

In the past several years, however, I have been questioning the certainty of my religious insider-outsider worldview. Such certainty had a tendency to divide my world and isolate me from the "outsiders," who, as some of my co-religionists and I believed, could not teach me, bless me, or correct me in the matters of God.

Now I am looking for a better way to stand on the ground of my beloved religion, to hold the treasures of my faith differently. Now I am looking for a better kind of certainty.

To create new empty space within, I decided to let some *uncertainty* enter my life, and I wish I could say the experience has been wonderful. It hasn't. It feels like stepping on a makeshift bridge, suspended, with firm ground left behind and no assurances of what I might find beyond the thick fog in the front. Questioning my own certainties has been a lonely, painful experience.

Uncertainty hurts.

Yet it is uncertainty that has been saving my life. Doubt would carry me. When I allowed more questions to serve as vessels of my faith, life could win. And expand. I could grow deeper, where fresh, strong new currents of faith could be found.

The thirteenth-century Sufi poet Mevlana Jalaluddin Rumi, a great scholar of ancient Scriptures, theology, and law, confesses:

> *Those who don't feel this Love*
> *pulling them like a river,*
> *those who don't drink dawn*
> *like a cup of spring water*
> *or take in sunset like supper,*
> *those who don't want to change,*
>
> *let them sleep.*
>
> *This Love is beyond the study of theology,*
> *that old trickery and hypocrisy.*
> *If you want to improve your mind that way,*
>
> *sleep on.*
>
> *I've given up on my brain.*
> *I've torn the cloth to shreds*
> *and thrown it away.*
>
> *If you're not completely naked,*
> *wrap your beautiful robe of words*
> *around you,*
>
> *and sleep.*[1]

Rumi doubts words, especially words about God, and trusts the experience of living instead. Not because words are a lie, but because in comparison with life itself, words that seek to explain life are sleeping pills. Our experience of living cannot be contained in mere language. Our formulations are shallow. Life spills over.

If you are drawn to stay on the solid ground beneath your feet, it might be best to follow that impulse and get rid of this book.

If you resonate even fleetingly with Rumi's ecstasy of losing confidence in words that attempt to define or deny God, read on, and let's take this difficult journey together. On the other hand, if you are drawn to stay on the solid ground beneath your feet, it might be best to follow that impulse and get rid of this book. The blessing of firm ground is hard won and, I now know, can easily be underestimated.

For me, the certainty of my own isolating belief system became unbearable. For a long time, I tried to deny it. I kept telling myself I had to stay faithful to what I believed. But eventually I had to be honest about what was happening to me and decided to face my fears of uncertainty.

A GOD WORTH WORSHIPING

I made it a personal discipline to take trips outside the boundaries of Christianity. I did it, first, to find out whether my God is on the outside of my religion, woven into all of life, and second, to look at my religion from the outside in and experience the way my religion, like any other, excludes others. In the process, I have adopted a simple question that helps me navigate the journey: Is a God who favors anyone over anyone else worth worshiping?

It is here, staring into this obvious question, that traditional Judaism, Christianity, and Islam often become paralyzed. Throughout history, we have been struggling with this. Today, however, *the other* is rapidly moving into our political, economic, physical, conceptual, familial, and emotional neighborhoods. We have never been connected like this before.

And like never before, the presence of the other in all of its beauty, fragility, dignity, and need is demanding our answers. If God created all humanity but gave life-giving knowledge—usually referred to as "revelation"—to only some of humanity, could God in any meaningful sense be thought of as the One God and not only as *a* god?

> *To say that God has decided to visit all humanity through only one particular religion is a deeply unsatisfying assertion about God.*

Wouldn't such a god be historically or geographically local and therefore either disinterested, powerless, or in some other way incapable of giving lifesaving knowledge to all humanity? To say that God has decided to visit all humanity through only one particular religion is a deeply unsatisfying assertion about God.[2] Once I made this opening in my heart, difficult questions began bursting out with startling force.

I began to reason that either every human being has a genuine opportunity to know One God, or God cannot in any meaningful sense be the God of all humanity. In other words, if knowing God is a way to life, and if God has divided the world by revelation, then the destiny of those who don't have access to a life-giving revelation of God would serve no other purpose than being a "control group" in a cosmic experiment, a vast human sacrifice. In even more stark terms, Yahweh, Abba (meaning "Daddy," a name for God that Jesus affectionately used), or Allah would not differ from Moloch, an ancient god of destruction reported in the Bible that required human sacrifice for his glory.

Most, or at least some, people would be created by God for one purpose—to die. Would such a God be worth worshiping?

> *Faith is an exercise in having high expectations of God.*

I asked myself, "Do we have the right to ask these questions about God? Can we question God's motives, wisdom, and ability?" and came to a conclusion that we have not only the right but an obligation. Faith is an exercise in having high expectations of God. Why wouldn't we ask? Our sacred Scriptures urge us to insist that God is light in which there are no shadows. Rather than offending the name and character of God, such high expectations actually honor God. It is the way we distinguish God from nongods, the way we worship God.

At times, we tell ourselves, "God is a mystery, and we cannot know God's ways. So the questions that try to explain God and God's ways are beyond our ability to understand. We are not

God, and we have to accept that we cannot know." I get that. I get that we can't get it. It's true, we cannot know God as God is. We are mere human beings. But these questions about God did not seem pointless to me. To say "God is a mystery" is too often used as a self-serving conversation stopper, effectively avoiding the task of addressing questions we don't yet know how to answer. We can keep our images of God safely unchallenged and protected from conclusions that might force us to concede the presence of God in people with whom we disagree. These questions, if entertained, might demand that we change our theologies, liturgies, and practices. The bondage of certainty can supplant the freedom of faith and make it impossible for us to say, "We don't know," "We apologize," "We want to change," and "What can we do to make things right?"

If we choose to interpret our sacred texts and cherished traditions in a way that fosters an image of God who withholds God-self from people outside our religion, would not such a choice make God not only less than divine but also less than human? Shouldn't God at least match our human capacity for justice and compassion? These questions haunted me all the way into a confession of my doubt. Either everyone has a real opportunity to find God, and therefore life, or God is not worth worshiping. A view of God who mysteriously withholds God-self from everyone fails the moral sensibilities of the general public and should fail the moral sensibilities of ardent believers. For God to create human beings to die in order to show the consequences of life outside Judaism, Christianity, or Islam is incompatible with the core teachings of Judaism, Christianity, and Islam. To think of

God as favoring any human group would be simply un-Jewish, un-Christian, un-Muslim. *A* god would take a place of One God. If God is not on the outside of our religions, whatever is inside is meaningless.[3]

Without God on the outside, the inside crumbles.

OUR OPPORTUNITY

I am not saying that it is possible or desirable to reconcile the religions of all humanity into one universal set of principles. Such an amalgamation would lead to the trivialization, dissipation, and ultimate loss of the treasures of religion and culture. The desire for common good and spiritual unity of all humanity often creates a mandate to impose these "obvious" universals on everyone. We all differ through our particular stories and ways of being. That we are all particular is what's universal about us. We have this treasure of difference, and our first valid response to this state of affairs should be gratitude.

It is also true that we cannot isolate our religions from one another. Total separation of our languages and meanings would lead to an equally devastating loss of the larger human community. The world communities of business, education, art, and science have been overcoming the isolation of human communities faster than our religions. My daughter's public school class is more religiously diverse than interfaith conferences I have attended. Religious communities today function as a kindergarten of toddlers in what developmental psychologists call "parallel play," playing *next to* but not *with* each other. Living parallel lives provides no synergy that can help mend our inner selves and the world.

By and large, our grassroots interfaith life consists of a series of events such as yearly concerts, meals, conferences, panel discussions, or worship services. When I walk into one of them, I usually feel as though I have walked into a prom party. People come dressed in their best, quietly observing, talking politely, standing in a new proximity to each other. It is all so awkward. When the event is done, we can finally shake hands and tell each other, "This was really nice. Let's interfaith again next year," and go home.[4]

> *The heart of a religion that will bless the world is going to beat at its edges.*

I am not arguing for a middle way in which two sides give up some of their meaning in order to coexist nor for an existence in which we stay isolated within our own meanings and never truly relate to one another. This book recounts my life journey toward a fourth way. I have become convinced that a God who favors me over others would not be worth worshiping. To truly care for me, my God also has to care for you. I will try to show that for religion to recapture human imagination, the theology and practice of *finding God in the other* will have to move from the outskirts of our religious experience to its center. The heart of a religion that will bless the world is going to beat at its edges.

We are realizing that our relationship with the other and our relationship with the Divine Other are inextricably intertwined.

Now we have the responsibility and right to seek and find "sacred space" outside the walls of our religions. What an opportunity! We have saturated our religions with our own selves, and the most direct way to enter a new whirlwind of fresh and substantive religious experience is to seek and find the image of God in those who are not in our image. It is really all about God, and God is really all about *all* of us.

THE COMFORT OF DISOWNING GOD

But to accept the presence of the ultimate truth, justice, and beauty in the other will be costly. To many of your or my fellow insiders, it will feel like disowning everything that our communities stand for—like a betrayal. When I became a Christian, my distraught atheist and Muslim family expelled me from home for two years. I was in college at the time, studying structural engineering, and came to depend on the kindness of strangers, moving from home to home. When I began to question the Christian fantasies of supremacy over all other religions, I had to make a difficult career decision and leave the security of a job in a large church and, with my wife and two young daughters, start our life again.

> *So much of who we all are depends on maintaining a polarized and conflicted world.*

That's why each one of us should think twice before we start taking these thoughts about the sacred in the other too seriously. Administrators of the organizations we belong to, be they liberal, conservative, or of any other stripe, won't know how to deal with it. Our families won't know how to deal with it. Our friends won't know how to deal with it. So much of who we all are depends on maintaining a polarized and conflicted world. To challenge this state of affairs by finding God in the other not only disrupts our communal sense of identity but also alters our social and economic structures on every level, from our families to our nations. In some twisted way, we have learned to benefit from the misery of the divided world we have created. Now we have to unlearn what we think we know and then learn to embrace this newfound reality of our globally intertwined community.

If you want to walk this path of challenging the truth you grew up with, the words of beloved Quaker author Parker Palmer can comfort you:

> Where do people find the courage to live divided no more when they know they will be punished for it? The answer I have seen in the lives of people like Rosa Parks is simple: these people have transformed the notion of punishment itself. They have come to understand that *no punishment anyone may inflict on them could possibly be worse than the punishment they inflict on themselves by conspiring in their own diminishment.*[5]

To continue indulging in the supremacist fantasies of my own religion would, for me, be to conspire in my own diminishment and in the diminishment of my religion. My journey with God would have to stop. There would be no future for such a God in my life.

The problem of dividing the world into outsiders and insiders besets all systems of meaning. I am not questioning whether we need boundaries to have an identity. Obviously, we do. I am questioning our practice of drawing the line between us and the other on the basis of possessing something that is not ours to possess.

It is dawning on us: none of us can possibly be in charge of God. German poet Rainer Maria Rilke wrote a poem that includes these words:

> Do not be troubled, God, though they say "mine"
> of all things that permit it patiently.
> They are like wind that lightly strokes the boughs
> and says: MY tree. . . .
>
> They still say "mine," and claim possession, though
> each thing, as they approach, withdraws and closes;
> a silly charlatan perhaps thus poses
> as owner of the lightning and the sun.
> And so they say: my life, my wife, my child,
> my dog, well knowing all that they have styled
> their own: life, wife, child, dog, remain
> shapes foreign and unknown,
> that blindly groping they must stumble on. . . .
>
> God, do not lose your equilibrium.
> Even he who loves you and discerns your face
> in darkness, when he trembles like a light
> you breathe upon, — he cannot own you quite. . . .

God, who can hold you? To yourself alone
belonging, by no owner's hand disturbed,
you are like unripened wine that unperturbed
grows sweeter and is all its own.[6]

This is profoundly comforting for me. The certainty of my personal belief system gives way to the God I cannot own, thus creating an opening toward a better kind of certainty.

The Anglo–Sri Lankan philosopher Ananda K. Coomaraswamy writes, "The modern Christian, who thinks of the world as his parish, is faced with the painful necessity of becoming himself a citizen of the world; he is invited to participate in a symposium, and a *convivium*; not preside—for there is Another who presides unseen—but as one of many guests."[7]

My experience has been that we religious people, particularly Jews, Christians, and Muslims, have been hedging our bets. We say we believe in the God of all people. But we really don't. We find it difficult to accept that others have anything significant to teach us about what we hold sacred, about our God. We tend to nod our heads at others only when they simply mirror what we already know. There is no reciprocity.

Yes, we are ready to defend the God we believe in. But can anything meaningful be said about God from a posture of defense? And atheists mount an offensive every once in a while. Fighting religion and religious people, these new atheists at times fall into the same trap along with believers, embracing a raging dogma entrenched inside their own circle of wagons.

"Though they say 'mine,'" as Rilke puts it, God refuses to be owned and to comply with our religious constructs, remain in our spiritual categories, or stay behind the walls of our theologies or ideologies. Has the time come for religious people to disown the God they believe in and for atheists to disown the God they don't believe in? That way our conversation about God will not be a way of building a wall that separates us but a way of talking and doing something about what matters to us, this miracle of difference and togetherness, now, on this earth. Done rightly, the act of disowning God would not be a betrayal of one's own religion or a worldview, but an act of gratitude to God and an affirmation of this beautiful gift we all have—life.

> *Has the time come for religious people to disown the God they believe in and for atheists to disown the God they don't believe in?*

Coomaraswamy also argues that the knowledge even the most learned religious people have about each other's faiths is virtually nil "because they have never imagined what it might be to live these other faiths. Just as there can be no real knowledge of a language if we have never even imaginatively participated in the activities to which the language refers, so there can be no real knowledge of any 'life' that one has not in some measure lived."[8]

On our intercommunicating and interdependent planet, the fences and distances that once allowed us to suppress questions about God's life among people of other religions are collapsing.

Our lives are intertwined, and our future hangs on our ability to set our eyes higher than peaceful coexistence and learn to thrive interdependently.

Now we live with the other, in our families, our workplaces, our neighborhoods. This whole planet is one big house. This is the end of parallel play. One after another, our religions and worldviews will continue losing their battles with life until we learn to respect what our experience of life together is telling us. Theology and the practice of finding God in the other will move from the outskirts of our religious experience to closer to its center. A better kind of certainty is within our reach.

Life will win. Life always wins.

And religion? It will have to lose its life in order to find it.

In the following pages, I invite you to take a reflective walk with me from scene to scene in my life. You are welcome to enter my story. And if I ever have the privilege of meeting you, I would love to hear yours.

1

LIVING WITH A SPLINTER

ONCE A YEAR, WE TAKE OUR TWO YOUNG daughters, Ena and Leta, to a cemetery. We visit dead people. We do it while on a vacation, usually on the Sabbath, in a town where we can't find a congregation that worships on Saturday. My wife, Vesna, locates the closest cemetery on a map, I prepare a picnic basket, and we put on nice clothes.

We look down at the tombstones. The fresh ones, the neglected ones, the well-kept ones, the forgotten ones. Tombs for Roman Catholic nuns, a brave fireman's mausoleum, a Muslim family's gravesite, a poet's tomb. The girls notice details of the portraits etched into upright-standing marble slabs. They ask about who brings the candles and whether they can pick the flowers growing around the edges. They run and stop in their tracks to watch a widow kneeling and cleaning the tomb of her late husband.

As we ponder the thousands of graves in thousands of cities over thousands of years, our minds struggle to imagine all the laughter and tears buried beneath our feet. Inevitably, the four of us wind up walking closely together, both girls settling down, holding our hands.

"Mom, Dad, what is a cemetery?"

"It's a place where we remember."

"Remember what?"

"Something we've forgotten since the last time we were at a cemetery."

"I forgot. What is it, Dad?"

"That life is a gift."

"Dad, maybe we could also visit a place where people are born."

"Yes, let's do that."

THIN PLACES

Christianity was introduced to Ireland without bloodshed, a process fairly unique in religious history. When Saint Patrick introduced his religion to the Celts around 431 C.E., he discovered that God had already been among the Celts before Christianity arrived. So instead of completely dismantling their spiritual experience, Patrick found presence of God outside the walls of his religion. He introduced the beauty of his faith as he learned from this often brutal but already spiritual people in the unique context of theirs and the result was a fresh

Christian spirituality, different from its contemporary Roman counterpart, that remains attractive to this day.

Celtic Christians sought after "thin places," spots where the membrane between mere physical reality and the reality of God's presence thins out and becomes soft and permeable. For them, thin places are locations in space or time where God's world ("reality as it really is") intersects with our world ("reality as we happen to experience it") so that it can be seen, touched, tasted, or sensed in some unmistakable way. They believed that at places like shorelines, fjords, rivers, and wells, the veil was so sheer, one could almost step through it.

> *The city is a sacred place; God loves people, and where people are, God is.*

For eight out of the past twelve years, the crowded city streets of New York City have been my thin place. I like to move from favorite people-watching spots in the city, such as Union Square Park, where people relax, to places where I can sit and watch them scurry to and from work. Although New Yorkers are burdened with heavy demands, their walk is as energetic and brisk as their lives. They move quickly and determinedly, pulled along by desire, suspecting—or, rather, knowing—that there must be something more behind the gray noise of the day made by humanity compressed into a dream factory the size of a city. Yet the city is a sacred place; God loves people, and where people are, God is. It is God's love that is compressed in this city, a thin place for the citizens who have eyes to see and ears to hear.

A thin place could be a conversation, a dream, a room, a tree, a dawn, a shore, a dance, a person, a scientific lab, a Sabbath, a Eucharist, an early morning meal before the Ramadan fast begins. Once, while I was teaching a class at a Christian theological seminary in Michigan, a young woman raised her hand to describe the experience that led her to faith. Years ago, in her room, while working on her computer, she turned to reach for a book, and it happened. She *smelled* God. That's what she said. You could almost hear the rest of us in the classroom thinking, "Oh, please. It is embarrassing characters like this that tarnish the reputation of Christianity as a respectable religion. Let's talk about something sane and real." But she was sane and real, lucid like the bright icy Michigan day outside of the walls of the Andrews University classroom. At her thin place, she caught a scent of God, and her life took a turn.

Thin places are stopping places where we, for at least a moment, step into what lies beyond the doorway of the world limited to our five senses. These experiences confirm our hopes and bind us to our beliefs. Two worlds become one.

THE ETERNITY PARTICLE

The Wise Man in the book of Ecclesiastes said, God has "set eternity in the human heart."[1] This does not mean simply that we want to live eternally but that we want to live an eternal *kind* of life *now*, within this present fragile existence of ours. We are used to dividing life—and God—into immanent and transcendent, into "here and now" and "there and then." In contrast, the Wise

Man argues that "there and then" has been planted in the center of "here and now."

Something or Someone lodged this eternity particle in our inner lives. The edge of the divine splinter tears into our mortal tissue. No wonder life hurts at every turn. We exist, but we want more. Sometimes it feels like a dull pain, sometimes a sharp cut, as spirit enters flesh.

That's how God blesses us. We attend to the part of the body where the pain is. We look at it over and over again. We touch it, wash it, cool it, warm it, scratch it, suck it, bite it, leave it alone. We try to forget about it. But to no avail.

Life is such an immense gift that inevitably we turn back to seeking more, that Something or Someone who gifted us.

Often this splinter feels not like God's presence but like God's absence.

We have all seen some of the ubiquitous reality shows on TV. "People are tired of virtual," say the media types, "so they want something real." A couple of years ago, my family and I were invited by a TV network to participate in a reality show where two families would swap a family member for a period of time. The producers thought that featuring a clergyman's family would be a great way to spice up the series. The offer was sweetened with the promise of $50,000 if our family was accepted.

It sounded great. Then we were faced with the groundwork required. To be considered for final selection, we had to offer a slice of our reality for the show and produce a home video in which we would "show our daily life in an interesting way." There was a two-page list of what that should look like. We were not asked to be as we are but to be more so. Although the TV people were saying otherwise, they were not interested in reality. True, we were not paid actors, but we were being asked to play parts. We would play ourselves.

Instead of leading us closer to the secret of our lives, reality TV hides it. My family and I were not asked to document the boredom, confusion, and uneventful aspects of our daily lives. We were asked to conceal such banalities by strenuously trying to be our most interesting selves. In contrast, the very secret of life is hidden in the ordinary, in its tediousness, repetitiveness, temporality, and inconsequentiality. My wife and I declined the offer and went back to our jobs, our laundry, and our bills.

> *Instead of leading us closer to the secret of our lives, reality TV hides it.*

As they hide reality from the viewer, these shows can be one of the many ways we dull the pain of the splinter of eternity, of the fact that human life as is, on its own, is merely a series of days moving along. The pain of human brokenness and suffering is nothing glamorous. Quite to the contrary, this pain that "eternity" inflicts on us feels like the absence of God. And nothing can hurt more than the absence of God.

But that's where an eternal kind of life always starts—in life as it is.

We feel this pain precisely because the Gift is now and here, among us. The pain of divine absence thus becomes a sign of divine presence. It is "off camera," in texture, sounds, voices, events, relationships, and experiences of the ordinary that God can be known.

God is.

If not here, then where? If not now, then when? Jesus would talk about *reality as it really is* as "the Kingdom of God" and would say over and over again, "It is near. It is here." All our lives, we live on this threshold between two worlds, the whole world as it really is on one side and the mere world of the five senses on the other.

And each life is a thin place in between.

OUR STORIES

The veneration of images is alien to Judaism. A commandment of God says, "You shall not make yourself a graven image, anything that is in the heavens above or on the earth beneath or in water under the earth." Nothing can therefore be *B'Tzelem Elohim*—in the image of God. No thing and no one.

> *The one symbol of God is a man, every man. And a woman, every woman.*

Yet Judaism (and the Bible) teaches that there is something in the world that is in the image of God. Not a temple, not a tree, not a statue, not a star. The one symbol of God is a man, every man.[2] And a woman, every woman.

God said, "I created a man and a woman in my *Tzelem*."

This teaching has numerous and immense implications, the main being that each of our life stories reveals God. The beautiful stories as well as the ones we would rather not tell, those that add an exclamation mark to the cries we earthlings direct toward the heavens. Regardless of our religious or ideological convictions, we all live by the hope that all of our stories together will ultimately weave a tapestry of love and meaning.

The Bible says that not all is well with humanity. Something went wrong. Something got broken. But it also says that the same grace that created us all is there to restore us. Jews would say that God's restorative revelation to humanity is therefore contingent on me and you, on our stories of creation and re-creation. God chose to pack his truth and beauty into us! Judaism teaches us that one can't know God without knowing humanity and that one can't know humanity without knowing God. That's why the Jews insisted on stories and not information as the premier way of knowing. No facts can speak for themselves. Every truth is dependent on a story, and every theology is a biography.

Today, living vicariously, we are becoming more accustomed to watching life through media than living it; we turn away from our own stories and the stories of people around us, as though they are what they seem, a series of days moving along. And thin places stay unvisited. Our imagination is becoming slothful; our fantasy lives are more and more alike, directed by professionals. Daunted by the work of finding immense glory in our ordinary individual lives and unexceptional communities, we hesitate to seek God in ourselves and in the other.

In fact, we are afraid to be in the image of God. And we are terrified of the prospect of finding the image of God in those who are not in our image.

But there is no way around the obvious glory of life that is within us all. No matter what we do, the splinter of eternity is not going to go away. The gift of life, in spite of death all around us, will reassert itself. So let's each one of us begin to say this around our kitchen tables, religious meetings, coffee shops, town squares, and chat rooms: "I am made in the image of God. I am made in God's *Tzelem*. We all are."

And then let us all tell our stories to each other. Here's mine.

ENJOY LIFE, AND DON'T BE A JERK

When my parents arrived in Zagreb, the capital of Croatia, from their small Balkan towns, they were teenagers looking for life in the big city. The '60s dances in their high school gym led to necking, then dreaming, then marriage. They were slow-dancing under the pictures of their fearless Marxist leaders and a big red star symbolizing the revolution, very much like American high schoolers dancing under the picture of a great American president and the Stars and Stripes. They staked their hopes on hard work and the strength of their relationship. My mom has a picture from the time: a newborn baby (my older sister) lying on the only bed in the first studio apartment they rented, a cooking pot on the floor collecting rain leaking from the ceiling. And there they were, my lanky father standing tall with pride, handsome; my mom with a fashionable oblong blond hairdo sitting with her hands clasped, thanking her good fortune.

We didn't believe in any of these religions or ideologies. We just lived. Well, we did more than just live. We loved life.

My dad's name is Sead because his family is Muslim from Montenegro. My mom's name is Marta because her family is Roman Catholic from Slovenia. We lived in the Socialist Federal Republic of Yugoslavia, which meant we were all supposed to be atheists. But we didn't believe in any of these religions or ideologies. We just lived.

Well, we did more than just live. We loved life. We had our own wonderful religion. There were two doctrines, unspoken, but as solid as any religious dogma can be. The first doctrine was called Pleasure: "Thou shalt enjoy life." In socialism, where we lived, we were not much distracted by the incessant marketing of consumer products. It always came down to relationships. And food. That's why our home always smelled good. It was a slow-food establishment with a spitfire-roasted lamb party at the end of the month of Ramadan—without fasting for a single day. We had a tree for Christmas and a roasted ham on Easter—without going to church. We made elaborate homemade European pastries on our country's holiday weekends—without ever visiting the Socialist Revolution Museum.

We found the best beef in the mountains of Bosnia; my father personally selected a cow every year to be sacrificed for our family faith, and we smoked it in a rented smokehouse. We made our own sauerkraut, had our own wooden barrel with prime cheese from Serbia, and for all the kinds of meat we could get our hands on, we had not one, not two, but three socialist refrigerator-freezers.

On weekends, from the time I was four, my dad took me to the marketplace in the center of our big city. He taught me how to buy the best food ingredients. We would come home with the car loaded with prime meat and vegetables from the countryside, and my mom and my sister helped us carry the treasure into the kitchen. Although we lived in a city apartment, on several occasions my dad would bring home a live chicken that we would kill in the bathtub. Talk about organic—and fresh! We all had cooking tasks, with frequent trips to the oven or stove to watch a stuffed calf breast roast or white Mediterranean fish broil or a walnut cake rise. As my dad and I knelt before the oven looking through the glass into our desire expanding and contracting under the heat, my dad would gently place his hand on my head, as though blessing me, saying, "Do you see it? It's breathing."

And there was wine-making. We carefully selected grapes every fall. It would be a one-week ordeal during which I had to cancel all evening outings with friends. All life unrelated to wine-making came to a standstill. Once the nectar was mature, we would bottle it, and over the next year, my dad would proudly bring it to the table for the endless stream of parties in our apartment. "If only we could find and befriend a Jewish family," we mused in a moment of self-consciousness about our abundance, "their passion would add even more zing to our celebration of life."

> *What mattered in life, besides pleasure, was to keep one's honor account in good standing and growing. Shame could nullify the honor and deplete the account.*

The second doctrine of our religion was Honor: "Thou shalt not be a jerk." One must be generous, honest, and hardworking—especially hardworking. Every individual and every family had an honor account. That was characteristic of most Eastern cultures. What mattered in life, besides pleasure, was to keep one's honor account in good standing and growing. Shame could nullify the honor and deplete the account. You gain honor by succeeding in your vocation, by winning the respect of others, and by having a family. You deplete your honor account by being lazy, deceptive, cheap, homeless, or without a family. For most of my life, filling my honor account meant studying hard. With good grades, I could do anything I wanted. My parents would pay for my sports and trips. For the honor that education brought, they overlooked some irregularities in the honor-shame structure—such as the time I dated my high school teacher or when I was caught smuggling pot from France into Germany during summer break. I was an honor student, and my account was in good condition.

I wish I had undergone circumcision (*khitan*) right out of my mother's womb or on the seventh day after my birth, as some *Hadith* (Sayings of the Prophet) say the Prophet Muhammad practiced with his sons. But in my father's family, raised in a Sunni strand of Islam away from the customs of the Arabian peninsula, boys were circumcised later, usually at age seven or ten, supposedly to mark the transition from childhood into boyhood. It was all done swiftly one summer day in the city hospital, and before I could walk comfortably, a party was thrown in my honor. Hundreds of close relatives descended on a ranch we rented outside the city for the festivities. Second and third cousins came. Never-before-seen uncles showed up. This was like Independence Day, a birthday, and a Thanksgiving party all rolled into one. And following the custom for such an occasion, everyone gave me money, which more than compensated for the pain of relearning to pee.

Only years later did I realize how important my big fat circumcision party had been to my father. It captured the glory of our family religion. Twin doctrines of Pleasure and Honor came together in perfect harmony. My father was the eldest son in a large family, and after his father and my grandfather, Zaim, died, he became a sort of patriarch for this carousing urban Muslim tribe. He was a savvy businessman and a charming leader. He left his father's home seeking a better life in the city, and he made it. Then he helped his parents, his siblings, and their families, moving them close to him where he could help them establish themselves. To top off the honor account, my mom was a relentlessly and at times recklessly compassionate and generous person, responding to people in need quickly and thoroughly. And my dad followed her lead. So they invited *everyone* to the party. On circumcision day, their only son turned into a boy full of promise for the world to see. The next man of the house was on his way! On that day, my father's past, present, and future came together. Life was complete. It seemed as if a lucky star had followed my dad from the beginning, clearing tragedy from his path.

> *My home religion, with all its scents, colors, laughter, hard work, and hugs, was for me a foretaste of an eternal kind of life I felt humans were meant to live.*

Until I became a Christian, and it all came apart.

My home religion, with all its scents, colors, laughter, hard work, and hugs, was for me a foretaste of an eternal kind of life I felt humans were meant to live. I would submerge myself in books, philosophy, and art, seeking *more*, then surfacing back into the grounded world of my family. Back and forth, seeking thin places, yearning for the two worlds to become one. And during my obligatory service in the Yugoslav army at age eighteen, I found the pearl I was looking for and became a follower of Jesus.

The sky fell down on our unsuspecting family. What the heavens meant to be a supreme blessing, they experienced as the greatest curse.

FOOLISH, NOT STUPID

My father loved life and lived with integrity, so people looked up to him. And as his only son, I was destined to inherit the mantle. After holding it in for a whole year at the request of my mother who hoped that my faith would somehow just go away, I decided to share the news with him.

He did not talk much about his feelings, and for this reason, we had never had a serious man-to-man talk. Every once in a while, he would dispense advice, as when he saw me struggling to stay in a relationship with a girlfriend in my high school and said, "Don't cling. Let go. You don't know yet what love is." But we had no serious conversations. I had never been in his office before this moment, at the age of nineteen. So to give him a clue and let him turn on his shock absorbers, I arranged for a meeting there. He was ready for some difficult news. Thinking back, I remember how confident he was when I came in. "An abortion? A totaled car? What can be so bad that the Selmanovic family can't handle! Bring it on."

After I declared that I had become a Christian, his body convulsed as if I had stabbed him in the stomach. If I had said I'd become a disciple of Santa Claus or Satan, it could not have been worse. In that moment, the world my father had carefully built over decades of hard work began to collapse. The news that his son had abandoned the family worldview and turned his back on the Muslim heritage and culture we were a part of was crushing. He turned away from me, lifted the chair he was holding to steady himself, and threw it against the wall.

A lot was at stake. Although my mother had assimilated into the larger Muslim family, really believing in God was never a serious option for either of my parents. It was questioning the unspoken doctrines of Pleasure and Honor that broke my father's spirit. He reasoned that if my faith had any basis in reality, his worldview was an illusion—and by extension, his life was an illusion. He couldn't accept that. Nobody can. But then if his worldview was rooted in reality, his beloved son was living an illusion, dedicating his life to an imaginary friend in heaven, another father. Either way, someone gets hurt.

My early Christian evangelical zeal did not help. I carried my Bible around with the confidence of someone who has just mastered the mysteries of life down to the last iota. In a society that had experienced the demonic side of Christian institutions and seen church history littered with hubris, oppression, injustice, greed, and slaughter, my wide-eyed drive to convert people made me a social nuisance. In a family that appreciated the joy of life more than most religious people appreciate their own religion, I was a heretic of the worst kind. But there was not much choice for me. Merely to survive as a believer in such a situation, I had to establish the boundaries of my faith with walls as high and as thick as possible. Certainty was the only way to survive—at least for a time.

Some of my relatives told me I had "betrayed family blood" by dishonoring my father and abandoning my Muslim heritage. I had never seen my father this devastated, with crying spells, yelling sessions, physical outbursts of rage, and propositions like "Run away from the Christians. Pick a country, a college. Just say the word. We will find the money." For him, religions were all about money and power, pyramid schemes of the ages. And his son was being sucked in.

In one of the last calm conversations we had before he severed my connection with the family, he said, "You are not stupid. But you are a fool." Then he paused, allowing his statement to sink in. It was an important distinction. He wondered how an intelligent being could make such a foolish choice. "Why would you do this?" he asked, and then pressed me by repeating the question, "Why would you do this?"

I was paralyzed by the presence of this wonderful and broken man whom I feared and loved so much. So I said, "I don't know. I don't know how to explain what I feel."

"Fuck!" he yelled—which is what I would have said, too, if I thought my son had lost his mind. Then after pausing and then repeating the word two more times, he insisted, "What do you mean, you don't know!"

I said, "Dad, Jesus says that 'those who have ears will hear.' I am hearing it. It is something so beautiful that it cannot be put into words. It is so present that I don't know how to explain it. It is like music that is coming to us from the universe and sustaining our very lives. The music of life's joys and life's sorrows. I hear it in the pages of these ancient books. Do you hear it, Dad? The music of life?" For a moment—I want to believe—he was intrigued by the idea, for he knew that life is difficult but beautiful, deep beyond reason. A gift.

ANGER INTO COMPASSION

Shortly thereafter, by order of my father, I was expelled from my home, my extended family, and my neighborhood. There was nothing particularly Muslim about what my parents did. In fact, it was religiously devout members of my extended Muslim family that softened the blow and provided support and love for me. In the city mosque, a man knowing of my situation opened the Quran and read to me: "There shall be no coercion in the matters of faith."[3] I buried this Quranic text in my newly Christian heart. It helped me resist the pressure to recant and let me stay the course.

> *I buried this Quranic text in my newly Christian heart.*

For the next two years, I moved between the homes of fellow church members, enjoying the kindness of people who were at once strangers *and* my newfound brothers and sisters. At the same time, I was realizing how utterly broken most of them were, their lives riddled with inconsistencies, petty arguments, and acts of self-righteous isolation from the world. For two years, I wandered around the city before I returned to the somber and tenuous atmosphere of my parents' home. They came around and accepted me, painfully—like parents who take in a gay son only because he is a son and never because of who he is as a person. "At least we tried," my family rationalized.

Returning home, I completed my degree at the University of Zagreb in structural engineering and in 1990 went to the United States to study theology. I quickly became immersed in American

Christianity, year by year realizing how self-serving the whole enterprise of organized religion was, irrespective of denominations. Religions were mirroring the cultures they were supposed to challenge, dismissing questions they did not know how to answer, struggling with one another for financial and political supremacy. And Christianity was not exempt. I signed up for a movement that was standing still, with explorers who had already arrived, and for a revolution that had given up.

I went to a spiritual retreat with Brennan Manning, a former Franciscan priest who collapsed into alcoholism and one of the people who spoke about the love of God in a way that helped thousands of pastors like me hang in with our respective church systems. He was a true evangelical mystic, helping us fall in love with God all over again. With religious foundations breaking under us and in God's sustaining embrace of daily life, pastors like me waited for the nebulous emergence of a new kind of faith to perhaps rescue us.

> *I signed up for a movement that was standing still, with explorers who had already arrived, and for a revolution that had given up.*

I coveted time alone with Brennan so that I could tell him about my frustration with the way my religious life was unfolding. I was angry. I wanted an explanation.

Eventually, Brennan and I connected at an event in the mid-1990s, and as soon as we were alone, it all poured out of me: "I am angry at my parents! Throwing their son out of the house? I am seething with rage, hurt, and judgment. And I'm angry with my church, too! When my parents abandoned me, my church summoned me before the church board to complain about the way I dressed. 'Concerned brethren' in Croatia wanted me to wear a suit and tie, a uniform placing me somewhere between a Western businessman and a Communist comrade!" I paused, but only for a split second. "I'm angry at the state of American Christianity! Was this it? Is the whole ordeal of becoming a follower of Christ worth it? Please tell me that this is not the whole truth!"

With his big eyes and bushy eyebrows, and in his confident way, Brennan listened in silence. Then, when I was done, he looked me in the eyes, and this is what he said: "So you're upset that they're broken."

Aghhh. His words twisted the splinter in my heart. The cutting power of his words made me realize that my experience with religion was not the whole truth. I, myself, and not just the world around me, was in need of deep repair. I had to go back to my life as it was, to my troubled and wonderful family, back to the frustrations and blessings of Christianity, and learn to embrace it all as mine. To this day, this deep repair is still going on. There are no shortcuts. At times I see glimmers of hope, my anger turning into compassion. Compassion for them—whoever "they" are—and compassion for me.

EMPTINESS

Back to the cemetery. And the birthing room. From the day of our birth, we all begin dying. And instead of regarding our very own precious life as a thin place where the Divine can be experienced, and instead of embracing death as an intimate part of life, every bit as much as birth is, we fear the end. Religious or not, we take that fear, make an idol out of it, and then spend our lives serving it. In contrast, the Wise Man in Ecclesiastes who wrote about the eternity particle being placed into our hearts also wrote, "It is better to be in a home where there is a funeral than in a home where there is a party." Why would that be?

Because death reminds us of our emptiness.

> *We fear the silence of the cemetery because in its spaciousness and quietness, we face our own emptiness.*

At the cemetery, there is plenty of empty space, and that resembles so much of the emptiness within us. But this emptiness is not something to be afraid of and run away from but rather something that has to happen in order for the Gift to enter.

The Bible opens with the statement that the earth was void and empty.

Then God came and created.

We fear the silence of the cemetery because in its spaciousness and quietness, we face our own emptiness. From silence we ask, "What if this whole faith thing is nothing more than a hunch? What if there is nothing but the tombstones above and the bones beneath this earth we are standing on?" And through these questions, an eternal kind of life begins. A space for boundless and abundant creation appears, a pregnant void. We become like fertile land where life is ready to sprout.

The last time my family went to a cemetery was during our visit to our home country of Croatia. We were all together, my wife, our two daughters, my dad now old and gray, my mom worn out by relentless care for us all, and me. We walked together. There was a Catholic section, a Muslim section, a Jewish section, and a section for atheists, great men and women of the Socialist Revolution. Our silence spoke loud as we looked back at our life. All of our religious and ideological boasting came down to this—an emptiness hovering over the green grass.

Why waste life (or another book, for that matter) on fear? You are in God's *Tzelem*, and I am in God's *Tzelem*. We are meant to live the eternal kind of life *now*. This kind of life will require regular questioning of everything we know, for we know so little. One of the greatest Israeli poets, Yehuda Amichai, wrote a poem titled "The Place Where We Are Right":

> *From the place where we are right*
> *flowers will never grow*
> *in the spring.*
>
> *The place where we are right*
> *is hard and trampled*
> *like a yard.*
>
> *But doubts and loves*
> *dig up the world*
> *like a mole, a plow.*

And a whisper will be heard in the place
where the ruined
house once stood.[4]

A place where we are right is seldom a thin place. Giving up being right about God, about life, about ourselves, is a process of emptying. When emptied of our need to be in charge of all the answers, we open ourselves to the stories of people we have always thought we knew. And as we listen and speak, we find our differing and difficult stories woven together, whole and beautiful, for the whole universe to see.

2

THE SECRET OF THE ORDINARY

I WAS EIGHTEEN, EIGHT HUNDRED miles from home, serving my fourteen-month obligatory term as a foot soldier of the Socialist Federalist Republic of Yugoslavia. One evening, hungry and with nothing to eat but a can of sardines, I needed some bread badly. Since no soldier in my unit had any, I went looking for Rajko Biševac, a nerdy-looking soldier with a big smile, known in the compound as "the Bag." The Bag was a Christian, the sort who would go around telling people how sweet the love of God really is—in other words, in the minds of most of his comrades, a troubled person. Soldiers and officers alike believed that withholding simple human respect from the Bag would help him come to his senses. So that's what they did. No perks, no promotions, and no approval of any kind for the Bag. Every once in a while, a zealous drunken captain who watched too many *noir* movies would take the Bag to his office for a smoke-shrouded night of pointless interrogation.

Moreover, the word was out that the Bag was not only a Christian but also a vegetarian, which somehow made him less of a man. To avoid the constant threat of being served food made with lard, he carried around a supply of what we all thought of as crappy food in a bag. Hence the nickname.

He didn't have any bread that evening, but each of us had something the other needed. So I approached him again a couple of days later. And then again and again. And as we talked, I came to realize that people were right about him—he was a fool. He believed stuff that was downright insane, but I felt I had a chance to help him out. There was hope for him, I thought. He was a fool, yes, but he was definitely not stupid. He put me on his prayer list. I put him on my crazies list.

The Bag was curious and full of life, laughing off the mean soldiers and paranoid officers as well-meaning and terribly amusing. He believed that he could change the world. That I could change the world. That anyone could.

By seeing it differently.

The Bag and I looked for ways to work the system so that we would be placed on tasks where our day could intersect. Even if one of us had to buff hallways or clean toilets in his own unit, the other one would be able to come and hang around. The only thing that mattered was that we could talk. The evenings, when most of the officers went home, were the best of times. Free from the judgment of other soldiers and officers, we strolled around the army compound, talking into the night.

"Don't you get tired of God?" I asked one evening.

He stayed quiet. Which prodded me on.

"Why do you always have to be thinking or talking about God? Why can't you just enjoy a sunny day, for example? Walk into the day and let it be, let it wash over you, with its own beauty, without *constantly* ascribing everything to God. You can't even enjoy a sunny day for what it is, can you?"

> "Why do you always have to be thinking or talking about God? Why can't you just enjoy a sunny day?"

In reality, the Bag enjoyed life very much. I was the one trying to come to terms with what seemed to me to be "God's oppressive presence."

He answered, "When I walk into a sunny day, I walk into a gift."

He implied that Someone actually thought about such a thing as a sunny day, that Someone "awared" it into existence.

Then he turned the question back on me. "When you walk into a sunny day, what do *you* walk into?"

I had no answer. In my mind, I thought of the ways a sunny day can be beautiful without attributing it to anyone, a product of a mysterious chaos from which we all sprang. But for weeks after our conversation, the idea that Someone gifted life to us would not leave me. The thought held me in its grip: Can reality be *relational*?

Later that month, I was working on something in the captain's office with another soldier when the Bag walked in. He seemed to be able to read social situations with ease, but the passion that he carried within him would burst out unexpectedly. Animated, he interrupted our conversation and began to explain something to my friend, apparently continuing a conversation they had started the day before. Standing in the middle of the room, he held an apple in the palm of his outstretched hand and looked in the eyes of my friend, then into mine and said, "See this apple? This apple is from God."

What if subatomic particles, atoms, physical forces, plant life, and brain chemistry are only letters? Letters that make words that make sentences that tell a love story about our world. An unbroken chain of the sacred lacing the ordinary.

The other soldier looked at the Bag as if the poor fellow had lost his mind. The Bag bit the apple, and the crunching sound, followed by a fresh luscious scent, filled the room. With his mouth full, he continued, "Did you ever notice that an apple has a different texture and taste at every layer?"—all the while chewing, his lips wet with drops of sweet nectar. "Did you notice, for example, how the apple is harder and a little more sour closer to the skin and softer and sweeter closer to the seeds?"

As he spoke in wonderment, I watched the green and red colors on the apple's skin waltzing together.

"This apple is a product of the love of Someone," the Bag concluded pensively and went out the door.

"The Bag is losing it," I said as I turned to my friend. My friend nodded in agreement.

But then I thought to myself, what if we are the ones losing something? What if we, not he, are maladjusted to the world? What if the world is not really made of mere random matter?

What if subatomic particles, atoms, physical forces, plant life, and brain chemistry are only letters? Letters that make words that make sentences that tell a love story about our world. An unbroken chain of the sacred lacing the ordinary.

THE FIRST GRACE

Fast-forward. After twenty years of pursuing an eternal kind of life as a Christian, I stopped going to Christian bookstores. Not because I couldn't find good books there. Good ones are still worth searching for.

It is just that Christian bookstores felt like places outside of life.

No matter how splendid the bookstore and no matter how exhilarating the experience of finding gems of Christian literature, when I walked out to the streets of Manhattan, I felt like my relationship with the city and its people had been put on hold while I searched inside the store. I felt like I had just been in a place where I reabsorbed a belief that God is about religion, that somehow this world is not good enough for God, and that God has decided to be confined to Christianity.

I had the same feeling when walking out of a bookstore offering the treasures of Judaica or Islamic literature or from a store selling Buddhist incense and bells. Whenever I stepped out into the street, I felt that the city's big, bad, wonderful streets and people had been left to fend for themselves. Religious bookstores, including those specializing in atheist or humanist sorts of books, have become like pharmacies for the human spirit, places where spiritual medicine is sold but life is not experienced.

The Bible never talks about "spiritual life," I noticed.

It only talks about life.

I have come to realize that the discomfort I feel at the door of a religious bookstore comes from God. Once, after walking out with a pile of Christian books I had purchased, I could not shake off the feeling that my life had been truncated into "spiritual life." So I turned around, went back into the store, and returned my books five minutes after paying for them.

"Is there anything wrong with the books, sir?" the clerk asked.

"No, the books are great. I just lost the sense of the presence of God by buying them, so I want to go back to where I was before coming here."

The lady behind the counter looked at me like I had three heads. With compassion. I seemed to her like one of those people Jesus would notice and heal. After walking outside, I prayed, "God, thank you for this city, this street, and these people around me. Grace did not start with Christianity and will not end with Christianity. It is a common thing in this world."

We are not only forgiven through grace.

We live by grace.

We even sin by grace. For without grace sustaining our lives, our sins would destroy us.

Like the air that surrounds us, touches our skin, enters our lungs, grace is unseen but real. And God is buoyant. Holding us without our aid or notice, much like what the Danish existentialist philosopher Søren Kierkegaard meant when he wrote, "Faith is like floating in twenty thousand fathoms of water."[1]

> *Our scriptural account of the world does not start with sin. The story starts with us being created. Sin came later. Grace came first.*

Nothing and no one *deserves* to exist. Whether by something as nebulous as chance or by something as nebulous as God, everything that exists was *given* existence. Free of charge. That's why our scriptural account of the world does not start with sin. The story starts with us being created. Sin came later.

Grace came first.

Many of us Christians have been insisting that we, with supreme revelation in our possession, are the only heralds and brokers of grace to the world. But as my friend the Reverend Vince Anderson says, grace has been seeping out of all of life, and others have been feasting on it all the same. We Christians have insisted that our revelation is the only container and only dispenser of grace. The rest of the world, graced from within, has been steadily proving us wrong.

Grace is independent.

Just yesterday, the Reverend Vince told me solemnly that the very last Christian bookstore in Manhattan had shut its doors. We shut out the world, so the world shut us out.

THE GREATEST SIN OF ALL

Kierkegaard reiterated a lucid insight of the historical church: apathy is the greatest sin of all because it means desiring nothing deeply and intimately. In other words, those who segregate the experience of life from the experience of the sacred lose desire. In contrast, undivided, the Hebrews loved both God *and* life. Obeying God meant being fully human, with every fiber of one's being alive. For the Hebrews, one could not experience one without the other.

Jalaluddin Rumi echoed the Jewish way when he wrote:

> *With*
> *passion pray. With*
> *passion work. With passion make love.*

With passion eat and drink and dance and play.

Why look like a dead fish

in this ocean

of

God?[2]

To our Jewish brothers and sisters, everything lives under the rhythm of God. Rocking their upper bodies back and forth as they pray, they tune in with all creation, with planets that move in rhythm around the sun, with the rhythm of our breath and heartbeat, as everything is linked to the rhythms of grace. They pray not to transcend reality but to embrace it. No matter how broken, difficult, or unjust, life is still a gift to us and is therefore sacred. To tune in to human life is to tune in to God.

Existence itself is a sacred place.

When I come across people who have converted from Christianity to Judaism, I ask them why. And the first answer I hear is one or another form of this idea: "Christians know how to talk about life, but they don't know how to love life."

ORDINARY JESUS

Dallas Willard writes about Jesus:

> If he were to come today as he did then, he could carry out his mission through most any decent and useful occupation. He could be a clerk or accountant in a hardware store, a computer repairman, a banker, an editor, doctor, waiter,

teacher, farmhand, lab technician, or construction worker. He could run a housecleaning service or repair automobiles.

In other words, if he were to come today he could very well do what you do. He could very well live in your apartment or house, hold down your job, have your education and life prospects, and live within your family, surroundings, and time....

The obviously well kept secret of the "ordinary" is that it is made to be a receptacle of the divine, a place where the life of God flows.[3]

Here is how Jesus lived:

Jesus woke up.

Jesus went to the bathroom.

Jesus ate breakfast.

Walked to the shop.

Opened the shop.

Took and fulfilled work orders.

Cleaned and closed the shop.

Walked home.

Cleaned and fed the animals.

Washed.

Ate dinner.

Talked to the neighbors.

Went to bed.

The next morning:

> Jesus woke up.
>
> Jesus went to the bathroom.
>
> Jesus ate breakfast.
>
> Walked to the shop.
>
> Opened the shop.
>
> And so on...

For thirty years.

Thirty.

Years.

Why did Jesus waste his life like this? If he could spread his teachings in Palestine in three years, why didn't he start earlier and go to China for three years and then to Africa for another three? The greatest teacher of life of all time—as far as Christians are concerned—the one in whom the Divine fully dwelled, spent thirty years of his life merely living. All that lost time. All that missed opportunity to change the world. So much wisdom not communicated. So much power unused. So much healing not done.

Why did Jesus waste his life like this?

Pity.

Why didn't Jesus use thirty years of his life to do spiritual things?

He did.

These *were* spiritual things. Sleeping, eating, working, talking, washing.

It is we who have shrunk the sacred. It is we who have segregated life.

By being like us, by dwelling in an ordinary life like ours, Jesus did not limit his influence but expanded it. He found grace at the roots of life. That's why the teachings that came from the life of this Palestinian carpenter spread in the world. Not enclosed in religion, he was "earth-wide" and "life-deep."

Because Jesus spent thirty years of his life doing ordinary things, for Christians, nothing should be ordinary anymore.

He was an earthling.

Among earthlings.

In the three years of his ministry, Jesus talked about life, not about spirituality. Even his lofty postresurrection utterances such as "Go to my brothers," "Make disciples of all nations," "Proclaim the good news to all creation," "Receive the Holy Spirit," and "Feed my lambs" were fused with the mechanics of daily life: greeting a frightened woman in the garden, walking down the country road talking to friends, eating a meal with his loved ones in the upper room, taking a keen interest in the life of fishing and the success of business, cooking breakfast on the shore, calling his friend Peter for the profession of his love. Jesus behaved as though grace is a phenomenon occurring not parallel to the rest of human life but as an integral part of human life, finding holiness in all that is secular.[4]

Parker Palmer asks about contemporary Christian faith over-loaded with abstractions: "How did so many disembodied concepts emerge from a tradition whose central commitment is to 'the Word become flesh'?"[5]

THE SACRAMENT

In Christian tradition, sacraments are formal religious acts conveying the grace of God to people, rites in which God is uniquely active. They are believed to have been introduced or instituted by Jesus. For many Protestants, there are two sacraments—baptism and the Lord's Supper. The Roman Catholic Church and the Eastern Orthodox Church have seven traditional rites that fit their definition. In a broader and more conventional sense, a sacrament is an outward, visible sign that conveys an inward reality of grace. Sacraments serve as doors (the "thin places") between the Kingdom of God and our world. Each religion has something that serves this purpose.

But instead of expanding our world and helping us find God in all of life, the sacraments have often been used to contract and divide. Vincent Donovan, a remarkable Roman Catholic missionary in Africa, challenged such practice: "A sacrament protects us and fortifies us with goodness. The more often we receive it, the better it is for us, the holier we are, the safer we are. And when we are finished receiving it, fortified and sanctified, we go back to that evil world, which just happens to be our human life."[6]

Our human life.

What if life itself, human and ordinary, is the supreme sacrament of all, a place where the eternal kind of life and the ordinary kind of life become one?

Over the centuries, many cultures in Asia have adopted a way of greeting, a gesture of bowing in *namaste* (India) or *gassho* (Japan), in which people greet each other by bringing both hands together, palms touching, in front, usually at the chest, or higher (below the chin, below the nose, or above the head). In this gesture, one hand represents the higher, spiritual nature, while the other represents the self, dwelling on earth. By combining the two, the person making the gesture attempts to show love and respect, to rise above differences with others, and to connect with the other person. This greeting communicates an understanding of the human condition in which two extremes become one. While the right palm denotes the feet of the Divine, the left palm denotes the head of the devotee. This union between two dimensions of human life is a source of the ultimate joy of life and solace for all sorrows.

The sacrament of human life is the sacrament that supersedes our religions. We live before we believe, and we are human before we are religious. Our life together is a temple where we all meet.

PEOPLE KNOW

Those of us who are accustomed to separating the sacred parts from the rest of our lives can't fathom how utterly unreal that way of living can seem to "ordinary" people. Take Christianity as an example.

People know grace.

They have been given grace already—a life. That's how they know. And every time people act in a truly human way, grace is there, active. When life bears hard on them so that they have to cry, or when life reveals its beauty to them and their breath is taken away, when they cry in despair or laugh with abandonment, or when they refuse to be embittered and take a road of hope, they know. They all know that these are remarkable experiences.[7] Hope is embedded in the texture of life itself. They understand. They see, touch, hear, smell, and taste grace.

What they don't understand is why many Christians are so bent on denying grace outside the boundaries of Christianity. This makes Christianity seem small to them, withdrawn from life, unappreciative of human experience, ungrateful.

An Eastern Orthodox theologian, Alexander Schmemann, in his book *For the Life of the Word*, offers a different and refreshing view of the Christian sacraments. For example, he describes the sacrament of baptism, in which the priest

> anoints the newly baptized, "on the brow, and on the eyes, and the nostrils, and the lips, and on both ears, and the breast and on the hands, and the feet." The whole man is now made the temple of God, and his whole life is from now on a liturgy. It is here, at this moment, that the pseudo-Christian opposition of the "spiritual" and the "material," the "sacred" and the "profane," the "religious" and the "secular" is denounced, abolished, and revealed as a

monstrous lie about God and man and the world. The only true temple of God is man and through man the world. Each ounce of matter belongs to God and is to find in God its fulfillment. Each instant of time is God's time and is to fulfill itself as God's eternity. Nothing is "neutral." For the Holy Spirit, as a ray of light, as a smile of joy, has "touched" all things, all time—revealing all of them as precious stones of a precious temple.[8]

A precious temple of life.

Jesus said that the hour is already here when God will be experienced and worshiped not in any temple made of human hands, but in spirit and truth.[9] By virtue of being human, we all have religion of some kind given to us by the community of which we are a part. That's why we need our religious words, symbols, and theologies. However, for our religious sacraments to survive, develop, transform, and serve their purpose in our interdependent world, we will have to abandon their role as enclosures of God. They are to become gates we can regularly use to help us enter a reality larger than our religion, the precious temple of life.

THE THIRD EXODUS

We are at the end of isolated Christianity. The end of isolated Islam. The end of isolated Judaism. The end of any kind of religion that poses as the "broker of the sacred."

As long as those of us who are Christians insist on staying enclosed in our own world of meanings, we have nothing more to say to the world. Without recognizing God, grace, and goodness outside of the boundaries we have made and without the possibility of expanding our understanding of God, grace, and goodness, we have come to a place where Christianity as we know it must either end or experience another Exodus.

In the original, First Exodus, God's people had many good reasons to stay in Egypt. Onions, for example.[10] Why move? Travel to a "promised land"? For what possible purpose? When Egypt is all you know, what could be better than Egypt! They were called to go to a land that had to be believed to be seen, which is the hardest thing people can do. They did it anyway. With great pain.

> *If those of us who are Christians do not find a way to acknowledge that God is everywhere, we might lose the basis for seeing God anywhere.*

Centuries later, the followers of Jesus had many good reasons to stay in Israel. In the Gentile world, they saw only darkness. What could they possibly learn from nations other than Israel? Could anything beyond Jewish culture shed more light on their path? Certainly, other nations could not possibly add to what they already knew. But they were called to leave their cradle. And they did it. Again, with great pain. But they did. That was their Second Exodus.

Today, millennia later, Christians are called to undertake another journey, the Third Exodus. If those of us who are Christians do not find a way to acknowledge that God is everywhere, we might lose the basis for seeing God anywhere. As Father Richard Rohr, a contemporary Roman Catholic thinker and author, argues, once we insist on drawing boundaries, once we have decided that the choice is ours and not God's, we have divided the world according to our preferences or, worse, our prejudices. He points out that we have "always decided and discriminated as to where and if God's image would be honored. Sinners, heretics, witches, Moslems, Jews, Indians, native spiritualities, buffalo and elephants, land and water were the losers. And we dared to call ourselves monotheists.... The Divine Indwelling, subject to our whimsical seeing, seems to dwell nowhere except in temples of our own choosing."[11]

We can either stay within the Christianity we have mastered with the Jesus we have domesticated, or we can leave Christianity as a destination, embrace Christianity as a way of life, and then journey to reality, where God is present and living in every person, every human community, and all creation.

Vincent Donovan prophesies, "The area in which the church must now find its meaning and live out its life is indeed, for the first time, the entire world. We can no longer think of anything less than the world." He says, "A gospel that is not as wide as the earth, that is without meaning for the whole earth, is no gospel at all."[12]

The world is rapidly changing, with growing numbers of people acknowledging our most sacred bond—that we are all human beings. Our consciousness as Christians cannot be separated from our consciousness as humans. The meaning of the word "sacred" is expanding, including ever more of life—one exodus after another—from bondage to a land, from a land to the nations, and now from the nations to all creation. The words of Jesus are being fulfilled: "Preach the good news to *all creation*."[13]

We can pretend that this journey does not have to be undertaken. We can pretend that Christian religion—rather than life—can be the ultimate arbiter of truth, justice, or beauty. We can pretend that others have nothing new to add to our understanding of God. We can pretend that we are above common human experience. We can pretend that we don't need the world.

But why would we? There is nothing to gain.

Except to avoid the great pain that accompanies every exodus. So herein lies the choice for those of us who are Christians. We can either stay within the Christianity we have mastered with the Jesus we have domesticated, or we can leave Christianity as a destination, embrace Christianity as a way of life, and then journey to reality, where God is present and living in every person, every human community, and all creation.

STRANGELY FAMILIAR

We are like sons or daughters leaving God to find God. At night in our beds, we think of all we can find if we take a journey into the world of the Spirit. So we leave the home of the ordinary and take off to explore, becoming ever more hungry for the ineffable truth and sublime mystery of God. Yearning, we move into libraries to read; we travel to places where we expect to find the Truth; we go to churches, synagogues, and mosques to submit, to pray, to learn, to believe. We seek God in the dawn, at the ocean, and between the stars. Our visions of spirituality, our visions of happiness, and our visions of ecstasy pull us forward like the music of a fiddler walking through our town. And if we keep listening to the music, if we don't get distracted by the competing noise, if we keep our vision clear and our heads up, we might at the end of a long and arduous road find the place we were looking for.

And... it will be the home where we started—the ordinary, secular, and mundane place that we left behind. It will be the bed where we began to dream, the home table where we ate. And the window by which we sat will have a view of the same street. We will come to understand that God was there all along.

For those who knock, the door will open, and the room they enter will look strangely familiar, made of the life they thought they were going to leave behind. The prodigal son and daughter will finally come back to life itself. It will all be the same, and it will all be different. That apple in the kitchen basket will now taste sublime, colors waltzing on its skin. Every bush will be ablaze with God, and no matter how broken, every person will finally be seen as made in the image of God, full of light escaping from the cracks in the heavy armor one thinks is needed for the journey.

Grace was first.

And grace shall be last.

The ordinary is laced with grace.

3

GOD MANAGEMENT SYSTEMS

MOST PEOPLE IN NEW YORK CITY CAN BE divided into two groups: those who use the city to make a name for themselves and those who are used by the city. Those who live here to love and serve the city are in the minority. I was not one of them. When I first came to live in Manhattan, I came to make it as a pastor. I did not serve the city; I used the city, and the city used me in return.

As evening edged into night, Gotham would cool down, dissipating the heat of the humans who had done battle with the city all day. Our family, too, would arrive at this time of respite, sliding into slumber without any unnecessary delays. But one night, a year after we came to the city, was different. Lying flat on our bed next to each other, with eyes wide open, my wife and I were confused and frightened by what had happened that day.

For six months straight, I had not taken a day off, and early that morning, I found myself in the emergency room of Lenox Hill Hospital on the Upper East Side with pounding heart, headache, and dizziness, hooked up to a system of tubes and monitors. Doctors could not tell me anything definite except to slow my life down or perish from stress. I was brought back home, and as Vesna and I were lying on our bed, I broke the silence and offered my wife an impressive set of reasons why I had been ignoring her pleas to slow down and take time off: difficult people in the congregation, shifts in history and culture that made religious work particularly difficult, lack of money, and that stupid, huge, ancient, rusty boiler in the church basement that nobody could fix. The list went on.

She was not moved. After I exhausted my list of excuses, she decided to love me in spite of the lies I had convinced myself to believe. So she told me the truth.

"It's all about you, isn't it?"

Silence.

Suddenly, my head was spinning again.

I was caught. It was not service for others that led me to the hospital ER but my ambition. I wanted to use the city, but the city wouldn't let me. Without knowing it, I had become my own greatest burden.

And I am not the only one. Those of us who are religious leaders seem to be hooked up to an increasingly complicated set of tubes to keep us alive. Everyone "in the business" knows this, and the dizzying pressure is filling the corridors of religious institutions. There are countless plausible reasons religious leaders give to explain why it is difficult for Christianity—to cite the religion closest to my experience—to thrive or perhaps even survive in the Western world. But blaming others for the troubles of one's religion is neither fair nor helpful. It is not about our aggressively secular culture or incompetent or unethical people who might govern our institutions or the lack of money and influence of the religious institutions. After all our church growth conferences, all our publications, all our evangelistic campaigns, all our celebrity preachers and authors, and all our ministries and seminaries, we find ourselves at the end of the day lying down next to God with eyes wide open, listing all the reasons for our misfortune.

But God is not fazed, one can imagine. God lies down next to us and our religion, listening, loving us in spite of our lies, telling us the truth.

"It is all about you, isn't it?"

> We want to use God to grow our religions, but God won't let us. And slowly, without noticing it, we have become our own greatest burden.

It is not the hard work of making the world a better place that has led Christians, Muslims, and Jews to exhaustion and constant fear of victimization in the vortex of public discourse. Many of us—religious leaders as well as believers in general—do ultimately make the world a better place. It is not about hard or effective work. It is about our ambition, the dream of actually managing God. We want to use God to grow our religions, but God won't let us. And slowly, without noticing it, we have become our own greatest burden.

TORN

As far as Christianity is concerned, I have noticed that many of my believing friends are, like me, spiritually fatigued. Not by the teachings of Jesus. Jesus' life still dazzles us, and his teachings still ravish us. Even the imperfection of our religious institution is not the issue it used to be. We understand that organized religion is like everything else in the world, broken and beautiful, fallen and redeemable. What perplexes us is being part of a religion that interprets its sacred texts, its history, and its practices in a way that confines and manages God.

On one hand, Christians cherish what God through Jesus has done *for* them and is doing *in* them. On the other hand, they feel that the Christianity that claims exclusive possession of God's revelation in the person of Jesus has hijacked that same God from the world. They feel trapped, required to fall in line with fantasies of the religious supremacy of

> *What perplexes us is being part of a religion that interprets its sacred texts, its history, and its practices in a way that confines and manages God.*

Christianity as a precondition for following the life and teachings of Jesus. They can't live without Jesus, but they can't live with Christianity. Jesus has provided grace and truth for them, while

Christianity's triumphalism has, openly or implicitly, denied the rest of the world that same grace and truth.

A weary friend of mine whose churchgoing has been steadily diminishing told me, "All my life, my religion has been teaching me two wonderful truths: first, that God loves me without any reserve, and second, that God wants me to tell others about and practice that same love. These two truths are not enough for me anymore. I want to find and love God in and among people who are not Christians. If God cannot be found outside of ourselves, then we have emptied the world of God! I have to make a turn here."

I hear similar stories from Jews troubled by a God who has left the rest of the world out in favor of the "chosen ones," as well as from Muslims troubled by a God who has locked God-self up in the words of the Quran. Have we turned our religious texts, traditions, and rituals into containers and dispensers of God?

> *Have we turned our religious texts, traditions, and rituals into containers and dispensers of God?*

A new generation of believers wants to find a God who dwells outside the boundaries of their own religious tradition, a God that would be worth worshiping. They are torn. They have discovered that God's presence or involvement with humanity is so obviously greater than their own religion. At the same time, they have discovered that the more they cling to their respective traditions of Judaism, Christianity, and Islam, in both their Western and Eastern expressions, they have to accept their traditions—without ever explicitly being asked to do so, of course—as God management systems.

MYSTERY OR ABSURDITY?

I used to think that God's choice of depositing the ultimate truth in my religion was a wonderful mystery. How glorious, I thought, that God would actually put together a religion to carry the ultimate truth to the world! Yes, others would have truth too, but not the ultimate one, I thought, thrilled that it was we Christians who were chosen for the top task. We were the ambassadors of God on earth.

Whoever has not tried this drink, I think, has never really been properly drunk. What can possibly compare to being in charge of God? Of course, we never said, "Listen everyone, we are in charge of God." Like drunks, we would deny even thinking such a thing, both to others and to ourselves.

My awakening began unexpectedly as I was preaching a sermon in a local church. At the time, I was at the university writing my doctoral dissertation. The library gave little offices to doctoral students so that we could be free from the distractions of campus life and delve into our studies. In this closed cubicle I would sit for long stretches of time, obstructing blood circulation in my body. The first signals of the discomfort appeared one month into the process, little itchy tingles at the end of my intestinal tract. I just fidgeted in my seat and continued the routine day after day.

After a couple of months of this, I found myself arranging for surgery that would cut, burn, tie, or otherwise eliminate the soft, bleeding pillows of excruciating pain on which I sat.

Whoever has not tried this drink, I think, has never really been properly drunk. What can possibly compare to being in charge of God?

A few days before the operation, I noticed in my desk calendar that I had a sermon to preach. It had been scheduled months ahead of time; I felt that it would be too much to ask the pastor to find a replacement at the last moment, and since I could not muster the courage to tell him the details of my situation, I honored the commitment. The topic of my sermon was "the glory of our God." I did lie down with my feet up for an hour right before showing up at the church, trying to lessen the pressure on the painful areas. I did the cream thing, and I did the alternative medicine thing. But to no avail. And now it was time to speak of God! I shook hands with church folks, hiding my predicament, trying to exude confidence. I walked up to the podium—smiled even.

And as I tried to tell people about God, I felt this utterly unbearable urge to leave the place and submerge my bottom in a lukewarm tub of lightly salted water, the only thing that would provide temporary relief. But no; there was no way out of this unholy holy task. I had to continue talking about God. God this and God that.

Until that day, I used to think of the notion that God has chosen to deposit God-self in our Scripture and the religion that surrounds it, and in us as a spiritual community, as a wonderful mystery. But talking about God while clenching a giant cactus in my rectum changed that. The situation was far more absurd than mysterious. I did not know whether to cry or laugh.

For the first time, I really understood the intensity of the American expression "pain in the ass." People could not make out why grimaces of horror would pass over my face each time I would move my hips slightly and weird smiles would appear whenever I would hit a good spot for an all-too-brief moment. I kept talking about God through that. Human talk about God became comedy, and at the moment, of a dark sort. That's how I developed my "theology of hemorrhoids." In a nutshell, it says that those who are not capable of admitting human limitations should not speak of God. Or to put it more bluntly, how can we humans possibly be in charge of God above us when we can't even be in charge of our situation below?

Has God confined God-self in our religion?

Apparently, many of us religious people think so, and whenever a thought occurs to us about how absurd that must be, we brush it off, and we say, "How great of God to pick us! What a wonderful mystery that is!" That is, until life sticks it to us and tells us that we are fragile and not in a position to be in charge of our own human selves, let alone God.

A WAY THAT IS GOOD FOR ALL PEOPLE

•

Jesus repeatedly said, "The Kingdom of God is here. Enter it." Jesus never said, "Christianity is here. Join it."

If a religion is going to be great, it must submit to something greater than itself, and Christianity is a case in point. To make it recapture human imagination as a "living faith," those of us who are Christians write and read books with titles that qualify "Christianity." The adjectives include "mere," "basic," "rediscovered," "authentic," "true," and "simple." I would not have become or stayed Christian without them. But no matter how mere, basic, rediscovered, authentic, true, or simple, Christianity is still not *it*, the Kingdom of God that Jesus, its founder, proclaimed.

Jesus repeatedly said, "The Kingdom of God is here. Enter it." Jesus never said, "Christianity is here. Join it." The two are not the same and can in fact, at times, be at odds.

Christianity and the Kingdom of God do have a relationship, but for any relationship to exist, a differentiation has to be made. Christianity is a religion. The Kingdom of God was, is, and will always be more.

If you are not a Christian, this differentiation may not seem radical to you at all. But for Christians, it is. A Jewish equivalent, for example, would be to say that only God can possess the land and that God is free to decide to share the Promised Land

and all other aspects of the covenant with someone other than Jews. A Muslim equivalent would be to say that God is free to speak before, after, and sideways of the Quran in a way that is equally or more clear and complete than all currently available interpretations of the Quran. An atheist equivalent would be to say that atheism is an integral part of all religion.

The first soul I "saved," a friend from my childhood in Croatia, told me after he was baptized and spent three years "in the fold" that "traditional religion is like an old, used-up, sick donkey. No matter how much you entice him, feed him, or beat him, this donkey is simply not capable of walking any further." I thought that was harsh—and untrue. I believe that traditional religion can walk in this world, today, and even run again. But on this one condition: it must be willing to hear—really hear—words such as these: "God is about the world, the whole world. God is about life, the whole of life. It's not all about you. It never has been. It never will be."

Most arguments of religious people boil down to a conclusion that the other is the real problem in the world, people who just don't get it.

Dallas Willard uses the term "divine conspiracy" to describe this effort of God that is larger than any of our religious undertakings. Religions, it seems, by and large see themselves as competitors or victims, not as collaborators. One way or another, most arguments of religious people boil down to a conclusion that *the other* is the real problem in the world, *people who just don't get it*. This exclusion of the other can, of course, be wrapped in humble and self-deprecating words, exalting God.

> *Religions are* meant *to lose their luster to God's larger presence.*

The claim of victimhood can be an acceptable stance for groups struggling for their interests or survival on the harsh stage of history. Empires come and go—and complain about the state of affairs beyond their control—all the way to oblivion, with nothing left but descriptions of their past glory in our textbooks. We can understand these imperial complaints because one of the roles of an empire is to outlast other empires.

But religions?

Religions profess that there is a reality above, behind, under, and within history. Religions are *meant* to lose their luster to God's larger presence. The purpose of religion *is* to be a servant of the world. A religion that refuses to lose regularly is a religion that excludes a greater context from its existence. Empires get glory, businesses get profit, artists get acclamation, and the governors get the last word. But from their beginnings, religions were not meant to be glorious, profitable, or acclaimed or to have the last word. They were meant to serve the world. And to be a servant of anything, one needs to accept not just the possibility but the certainty of being wronged, used, and forgotten. One must accept the burden of these outcomes as a part of one's chosen identity.

Rabbi Abraham Joshua Heschel expressed the importance of "one person" and "a moment" for any religion when he wrote, "When God becomes our way of thinking we begin to sense all humanity in one person, the whole world in a grain of sand, eternity in a moment.... [When] in the afterglow of religious insight I can see a way to gather up my scattered life, to unite what lies in strife; a way that is good for all men as it is for me—I will know it is His way."[1]

Christians ask, where is the respect for the uniqueness of Jesus in all of this? Muslims ask, where is the respect for the role of the glorious Quran in all of this? Jews ask, where is the respect for Jewish history and land in all of this? Atheists and humanists ask, where is the respect for human agency in all of this? Heschel answers all of us with a question: "How is your religion 'good for all people'?"

POSSESSING THE KINGDOM OF GOD

The identity of most religions and ideologies is tied to the claim that the whole world is in need of something they possess. Let's take the relationship many Christians have with the person of Jesus as an example. Many Christians believe that the Kingdom of God that Jesus spoke about is inseparable from knowing the person of Jesus. If so, the question begs to be asked: Is the Kingdom of God present in all of life, among all people, throughout history, or is the Kingdom of God limited to the historical person of Jesus and thus absent from most of life, most people, and most of history?

The answer to this question depends greatly on whether Christians are willing to make their religion take a backseat to something larger than itself.

My friend Sean Evans is a psychologist at the country's foremost institution for the criminally insane, Patton State Hospital, in Highland, California. It is a complicated workplace, a crossroads of high-flying emotions, a knot of bureaucratic governmental forces, criminal and insane behavior, and tender stories of people entangled in it all. People like Sean don't have the luxury of nicely packaging their communication. When in church, Sean has a way of saying things that cut through the ambiguities, giving voice to truths that are widely sensed but rarely expressed.

> *"Did someone just blaspheme?" We felt like running for the windows, jumping out of a ship sinking into an abyss of heresy.*

So when he said to a group of our church members, "The cross has become a Christian fetish," at first each of us thought to ourselves, "Did someone just blaspheme?" We felt like running for the windows, jumping out of a ship sinking into an abyss of heresy. Saying this kind of thing about the cross in the church can get both one's faith and one's social standing in church in real trouble.

But there was no doubt that Sean's observation was honest and well-meaning. Once it entered our thinking system, there was no way to ignore it. As soon as I got home, I Googled the word "fetish."

Used by adherents of voodoo, Indian tribes, cults, and witches in the form of an amulet, a talisman, or a lucky charm, a fetish empowers the person who possesses it. Similarly, we can think of the cross as something we can hold in our hands, carry around our necks, hang on a wall, and put in a box. But carrying a cross around is not a problem. Possessing a metal, wooden, or leather cross has been a meaningful spiritual tool throughout Christian history.

There is another way of possessing the cross, however. By "possess," I don't mean simply that we can buy or sell it, hold it in our hands, discard an old one and create a new one. The problem of possession arises when we Christians fancy ourselves as the sole custodians of what the cross stands for.

Thus one definition of "fetish" among several that my friend Sean had in mind and clarified on the phone for me the next day was that fetish is "a part of a whole that we imbue with the power of the whole and that we use to gain a sense of control over the whole."

The cross of Jesus was an event-object bound within time and place, recorded and preserved by those of us who cherish the Christian story. For us, it is not just a distinctive aspect but the central chapter in the story we tell, carrying multiple rich facets of meaning.

However, we have to ask, did something *in God* change when Jesus was on the cross? Was God's love toward us released by the cross, or was the cross an expression of love that is there at all times and places?

Was what was true about God on the cross true only at the cross? Or was what was true about God on the cross true about God among all people?

Would an event-object that empties most of space and time of grace and truth and deposits them into one story of one people be worth cherishing?

Did the custodians of the story of the cross imbue this story with the power to contain the whole of God, thus finally reaching a place where they have actually become the managers of God, holding the only set of keys to universal truth for everyone else?

Understandably, the custodians of the teaching about the event-object of the cross cannot easily see or accept the perspectives of those who were left out of this privileged transaction by virtue of when and where they were born or whatever kind of a teller of Christian story they happened to bump into. Christians like to talk about the "scandal of the cross," the fact that the suffering of a man (who was God or in whom the Divine fully dwelled, depending on which Christians we are talking about) in a particular time and place in history is the way God has revealed God-self. Christians find this scandal of suffering, humility, and love immensely reassuring simply because they are on the receiving end of this beautiful paradox.

I have come to believe that the cross is unique not only because it is local and historical but also because it is a window into something cosmic and universal. God experiences death with every injustice, oppression, and suffering. God has chosen to suffer with us ever since suffering began and does so with all creation and at all times. The birth, life, death, and resurrection of all that is truly good has been taking place before the term "Christian" or the phenomenon of "Christianity" was ever dreamed of. For me, therefore, Jesus is not only Christian but also cosmic, woven into all of creation and all of life.

> *I have come to believe that the cross is unique not only because it is local and historical but also because it is a window into something cosmic and universal.*

The birth, life, death, and resurrection of Jesus is, for me and my community, a window into the essence of God; into who God was, is, and will be; our shared thin space.

The cross is our treasure. Not our fetish.

Worship of the cross as a fetish insists on a vacuum of grace in the world. Instead of recognizing grace in all of life, in all places, and among all people, it constantly argues for its absence. The pain that this statement causes to the custodians of the cross story can only be matched by the joy of those who have discovered that the love embodied in Jesus is not in the possession of Christians but woven into the texture of life itself. Love, grace, and forgiveness are the way of God's world, not just the Christian world.

> *To claim custody of God and God's blessings is not only a Christian phenomenon. Can God's covenant with Jews be a fetish used against other nations? Can the Quran be a fetish used against Allah? Can science be a fetish used against the earth?*

A sense of control over the whole of God is attractive to us creatures riddled with uncertainties. In the long run, however, it is this grip of lust for control over the whole of God that undermines our faith. Mystery of religion that casts itself as God's broker to the world ultimately deteriorates into absurdity. Dallas Willard, who is a respected evangelical Christian philosopher, has astutely observed that many churches actually exist for the purpose of avoiding God. God can become someone safely contained by the words of our theology and tamed by the motions of our liturgy. In this arrangement, one can achieve one's own human purposes with professedly divine power and sanction. One is free to pursue a kind of life one would live without God, but with "God's blessing"!

This is hard to give up.

To claim custody of God and God's blessings is not only a Christian phenomenon. Can God's covenant with Jews be a fetish used against other nations? Can the Quran be a fetish used against Allah? Can science be a fetish used against the earth?

BLIND TO OUR OWN TREASURES

Moreover, fetishes overpower us and make us blind to the treasures of our own religions. That's why we need the other, who can look at our religion from the outside and help us see.

When I sought to rent an apartment in Manhattan a couple of years ago, I met a real estate broker (in New York City, one may lease rental property only through a broker) who was a Jewish woman. Walking through the city from one showing to another, I told her about my intention to try to bring together Jews, Christians, and Muslims in a community of communities where we could learn to be interdependent. She responded, "That's a great idea! I think Jews and Christians can be together!"

"And Muslims," I added.

"No, no Muslims!" she countered immediately. "They can be nice and pretend to be your friends and all, and you begin to trust them, and then they blow themselves up, you know. They're ticking bombs!"

I told her that I grew up in a Muslim family and that in the former Yugoslavia, Muslims were peacemakers who saw violence as a failure to submit one's life to Allah. I told her I had never seen a Muslim relative or friend initiate or retaliate with violence. Violence was beneath them, a sure way to dishonor oneself and God. To kill would be to take a life one cannot replace and hence to which one has no right.

I told her that before the war in Bosnia, we had our own version of *Saturday Night Live* that all of Yugoslavia watched, that everyone was glued to the TV at eleven o'clock Saturday night, eager to share the communal experience of late-evening belly-trembling laughter, and that the cast of comedians in Sarajevo consisted mostly of Muslims. In the explosive Balkans, no group of people knew how to make fun of themselves as well as they did, and nobody else was as trusted as Muslims to poke fun at all others.

"That's my experience of Islam," I said. "Am I a ticking bomb?"

> *"I want to go deeper into my religion, but at this time, I have only two pillars to my Jewishness: fear of another Holocaust and fear of losing the land of Israel. These two are not enough to sustain a religion."*

She had nothing to say. She had her stories; I had mine. But over coffee at the end of that apartment-hunting afternoon, she confessed, "I am Jewish, and I am afraid. I remember the pictures of the Holocaust that I saw while growing up. Adults warned me about the lessons of history, and the fear never left me. The world wanted to destroy us, and I was told that our suffering is different from other people's suffering. Others don't understand. I travel to Israel, and I see fear there. I want to go deeper into my religion, but at this time, I have only two pillars to my Jewishness: fear of another Holocaust and fear of losing the land of Israel. These two are not enough to sustain a religion. I need a Judaism that goes deeper."

I told her that from my perspective, Judaism does go deeper. Much, much deeper. It goes all the way to the marrow of life where the ugliness of human experience mixes with its glory. I told her that Jews have a gift for all people, especially for Christians and Muslims. Literally, "Israel" means "the one who wrestles with God." And don't we all? I went on and on listing the ways Judaism has nurtured and made me, including the fact that ever since I became a Christian twenty years ago, I have been observing Sabbath every week, sundown Friday to sundown Saturday. My Christian faith would never survive without Judaism.

> *My Christian faith would never survive without Judaism.*

"Your blessing is immeasurably larger than your fear," I told her.

And her eyes lit up.

CRAZY MUHAMMAD

Life interrupts us. When we can't fit our life experience into our religion, something has to give, and life can't give.

Like a sturdy surgical tool, life cuts back across our religion to save us from it. Just when we figure everything out, when our belief systems, traditions, and practices are beginning to play along nicely like a well-trained and tuned symphony orchestra, we stumble across something—an experience, a fact, a person. And nothing defies our religion so much as finding the sacred in one of "those people." You meet a Muslim man who resembles the character of Jesus more than anyone you've ever met in your church. You find yourself working with a Wiccan woman who is repairing the world better than anyone in your synagogue. You meet an evangelical Christian college student who puts everything on the line to protect the rights of atheists on campus. An atheist wise man or woman comes alongside you and helps you persevere on your path of faith in God. In such encounters, to use the poetry of Yehuda Amichai again, the moles and plows of love soften the stomped soil of a hard ground where we are right.[2]

That's what happened to me.

When I became a Christian, my devastated parents recruited one of Europe's best psychiatrists and fifty relatives to take their best shot at helping me get over my infatuation with God. Even my former girlfriends were summoned to try to evoke sweet memories and prevail over my heart. My mom was on stress medication, and after a couple of months, her face was scarred by an unending stream of tears. For the first time in my life, I saw my father cry. Everything evaporated; the pride about Christian institutions, the good deeds of my church, and the virtues of the Christian path were all deconstructed by a little army of people zealously researching the private lives of the members of my church. I knew which married Christian man had a woman on the side, who stole tools from the workplace, and who did not pay back a loan to a neighbor. After two months of this agony, my body and my spirit were giving in, and seeing my family suffer so much jolted me like nothing else ever did. I was tired, hanging on solely to the cross of Jesus, the clearest expression of God's compassion for me.

My parents did not sense my weakness at the time. Like me, they were on the brink of exhaustion, so they resorted to desperate measures and asked a religious person for help. They invited Imam Muhammad, a man respected in the Muslim community of the city, a "holy man," to attempt to throw my Christian belief system into disarray and stir me toward Islam, which in my parents' reckoning was the lesser of two evils.

When Muhammad walked into our home, somehow I felt safe in his presence. Besides being learned in the matters of Scripture, he was the most environmentally progressive and socially conscious person I have ever met before—a vegan who walked to our home from a far part of the city, avoiding transportation on principle, to protect the environment. A small gray-haired man with a large smile, Muhammad was emanating peace and playfulness, something my family needed so much at the time.

After being introduced, he kindly asked my parents to leave the room so that he and I could be alone. In spite of his kind manners, I still expected an attack, something I had heard dozens of times before: "The Torah and the New Testament are an incomplete mishmash of texts redacted by humans, whereas the Quran was recited by God and is therefore perfect, correct in all ways, superseding, and conclusive of all revelation! Come to the winner!" Instead, after initial small talk, he let time pass in silence, and I enjoyed this rare moment of rest. When I was ready, I raised my eyes and looked at him, dreading the inevitable argument. He stood up quietly, walked over to me, sat down, and lightly touched my shoulder for a moment.

Then he said calmly, "I am glad you are a believer." And nothing more.

After sitting in peace for a little longer, we stood up, and he opened his arms to invite an embrace. I opened mine. He smelled like wooden furniture and soap—old but fresh. Hugging him, I thanked God for giving me this break in life.

Neither my parents nor I knew what to do with what had just happened. After he left, my parents nicknamed him "Crazy Muhammad." My parents fell into a deeper despair, and word of Muhammad's foolishness spread in the family.

The grace and truth I had first met at the cross were embodied in this man, who was willing to be taken for a fool in order to make me whole.

Would I be a Christian today without Muhammad's blessing?

Would I have stayed in ministry without Soo the witch's blessing?

If Soo and Muhammad did not speak, God would make stones talk to me, I believe. Largely because of this experience, decades later, I got over my fantasies of Christian supremacy and signed up for the Kingdom of a sovereign God who is Spirit and cannot be controlled and, like wind, blows wherever it pleases.[3]

EVOLVING MONOTHEISMS

"I'm glad you are a believer." What did Brother Muhammad have in mind? I certainly did not become a Muslim. And as years passed, I became a Christian pastor and baptized many in the name of the Father, the Son, and the Holy Spirit. Definitely not a Muslim thing.

Believer? Did Muhammad sense that there is something to believe in, something larger that transcends or underlies our beloved religions?

God. God is greater than our religions.

> *Monotheism at its best stimulated us to imagine the world where every human being has equal rights and every life is sacred.*

Monotheists have been a blessing to the world. At their beginnings, Judaism, Christianity, and Islam were transforming the oppressive social order in their own societies. That there is one God meant that none of us were gods. And because none of us were gods, the life of each person was as sacred as the life of another. This basic concept of equality in terms of our inherent limitations allowed us to conceive of societies that would supplant the systems of revenge and oppression with mechanisms of protection, care, and justice for all. None of us has an absolute right over anyone else. None of us is self-sufficient. Awareness of our common creaturehood and our common life under the same mystery opened a new and radical path for respecting the other, no matter how much the other differed in possessions, status, race, gender, religion, or other accidents of birth. Monotheism at its best stimulated us to imagine the world where every human being has equal rights and every life is sacred. The awareness of this common origin of every person has helped change the world for the better, leveling the field, all the way to creating the basis of modern democracies. None of us are gods, and none of us can have unchecked power over anyone else.

The prophets of Israel, Jesus and the early church, and the Prophet Muhammad and his community in Medina demanded honest self-criticism and the embrace of the radical equality of all humanity. At our beginnings, we were all charged to find a way that is good for all people.

Yet monotheists have been a curse to the world. Instead of living out the gifts of liberty and equality embedded in the monotheistic faiths and instead of empowering the dissidents—our own prophets!—to challenge our prejudices and confront our shortcomings, monotheists have used the idea of God to turn on others. Instead of cherishing the prospect of living together under one Mystery and therefore in constant awareness of our limitations to manage it, monotheists have decided to impose their certainties on others. The circles of inclusion became smaller and smaller. Each monotheism in its own time and in its own way has sanctified egotism, justified violence, and fomented hatred. And done this to please God! As Karen Armstrong puts it in *A History of God*, "It makes God behave exactly like us, as though he were simply another human being."[4]

For years, I've been talking about the three monotheistic religions to nonbelievers. And here is what I hear: "At best, Jews, Christians, and Muslims look like three religious stooges in a slapstick comedy. At worst, they look like three brothers with hands clasped in prayer and soaked in blood." We have littered history with incredible amounts of stupidity, injustice, and suffering.

In every relationship, there comes a threshold when mere apologies will not do anymore. It seems we have crossed that line.

The world has simply had it with us. Nobody's listening anymore. Until we reembrace the limitations of our own creaturehood, we have nothing more to say or do to make the difference we were meant to make in the world.

The mission is over. Monotheism will either die or evolve.

DECOLONIZING THE NAME OF GOD

Monotheism can, must, and will evolve. The only question is whether we, the three greatest hopes and three greatest disappointments of history, will come to our senses, decolonize the name of God, and accept being part of something larger than ourselves. Or will we continue *using* the world instead of *serving* it, thus diminishing our God and ourselves in the process?

Religion is in trouble. If we cannot move beyond our "all-encompassing" views of God, if we cannot hold something more sacred than our own understanding, if we cannot have a sense of creaturely self-doubt about the way we understand not only God but anything at all, we all have failed the world we are supposed to serve, each through our own religion, and the only solution left is to battle this out and see whose God is bigger.

If there is nothing we can aspire to better than Christianity, Islam, Judaism, Hinduism, or atheism, a bloodbath then seems inevitable. Since human life without our particular fetish is not worth living, why not end it?

Each of our three Abrahamic religions makes two claims. First is the claim we agree on: "God is One." Second is the claim we deny we are making: "We are in charge of God." We are denying it because admitting to have One God in our own custody would amount to our being gods above God, which would be a betrayal of the first claim. Quietly, over the ages, our religions have colonized the name of God and become God management systems.

> *Each of our three Abrahamic religions makes two claims. First is the claim we agree on: "God is One." Second is the claim we deny we are making: "We are in charge of God."*

FAITH BREATHING

But regardless of how dismal the situation looks these days, there is hope. There is a solution. And it is not to stop going to our churches, synagogues, mosques, temples, libraries, bars, and other places where our worldviews are shared, challenged, and affirmed. Our convictions need to be deepened, not watered down. Our communities need to be blessed, not abandoned. The way out of this mess is being dug by people who are ready to live interdependently instead of self-sufficiently, undermining a classic myth of what it means to protect oneself and one's own people, taking the weapons—literal, psychological, political, or religious—and then defeating and conquering the other.

We have no more wars that can be won. The earth is reeling under our jostling for power. Empathy, cooperation, and forgiveness are becoming the most potent agents of transformation. We will be led by people who are able to help us measure our religions and lives differently, who refuse to reduce others to an enemy, who can teach us to turn our back to fear, who can strengthen our ability to forgive and absorb injustice instead of deflect it back into the world.

People want God, but not one who is the captive of a religion. They want an unmanaged God. Free God. That's where hope comes from.

> *People want God, but not one who is the captive of a religion.*

We have created a vacuum in the world. But in emptiness God is giving life to a new kind of faith, a new beginning. Any religion, when conceived as God's privileged faith with a mission to supersede all others, usually resorts to use of any means necessary, which amounts to aligning with sources of power in the world—political, economic, military, governmental. Historically, these powers were associated with masculine characteristics of superior physical strength, competition, and conquest. In contrast, this new kind of faith might be better described as a woman—not less powerful, just more tuned into the connectedness of all life. Perhaps faith has always been like a woman, and it is only now that we can acknowledge it.

A friend e-mailed me a picture taken in Israel of a wall that separates Muslim and Jewish people. On it, in red spray paint, a hopeful person wrote the words of Arundhati Roy:

> *Another world*
> *is not only possible, she's*
> *on her way. Many of us won't*
> *be here to greet her, but*
> *on a quiet day,*
> *if you listen carefully, you*
> *can hear her breathing.*

For another kind of world, we need another kind of faith. Now we have another kind of world. Religions that will thrive and bless us in the future will be "religions for one." This is not a call to one religion for all. It is a call for every religion to find a way that is good for all people, for we humans all belong to each other.

When we listen carefully, we can hear a new kind of faith breathing. She is already among us.

4

WHY IS GOD NOT MORE OBVIOUS?

WE WERE THE LOWEST FORM OF LIFE in the Yugoslavian army. Other soldiers referred to us infantry soldiers as "army peasants," "lizards," and "dust eaters." That summer evening, after the punishing Macedonian sun had finally set and before we were ordered to lie down and fall asleep, we cleaned the barracks floors, our boots, our weapons, and our feet, faces, and teeth. Like every other night, we did the chores hastily to save minutes for writing a letter, making a phone call, listening to the radio—anything to help us restore an awareness of the larger world outside.

I walked from the barracks over the vast asphalt runway, across the low brush field, and toward the woods, as far from the sounds of army life and as deep into solitude as possible. I did not want anyone to hear what I was about to say.

I went far enough to sense the hush of the dark woods before me. At the edge of the forest, I found an old wooden bench in a patch of weeds. An officer and his unit might have built it long ago when this part of the compound had served a different purpose.

It reminded me of a city park bench, six hundred miles away and six years back, where I first kissed Sonja, my first love. We were both in middle school, trembling at the thought of being alone by ourselves. We walked and talked our way toward a secluded corner of a neighborhood park, sat down on the park bench, and quietly waited for one another. I summoned my courage and leaned my head close to her neck, inhaled the scent of her skin, heard her breathing, and then placed my lips on the edge of hers. Sweet. I tasted the unfolding ecstasy of desiring and being desired.

She kissed me back.

What would happen now?

On that evening away from the other soldiers, sitting on that bench between two worlds, something happened not unlike my first kiss with my first love. Instead of facing my fears of making my heart vulnerable to the mystery of a woman, I faced my fears of making my life vulnerable to the mystery of God.

In the cool of the day, I sat down with the noise of life in the distance behind me, the silence of the forest before me, heat from the hot dirt under me, and the open sky above me. I was surrounded. And invited to surrender. My beating heart was responding to the overtures of God. The mystery of what I had read and heard in the Bible for the previous several months wooed me to this place, and I was about to utter my first prayer.

I did not know what to say. I just had to say it.

Faith sat on the bench beside me. She had been close to me all my life, but that evening, for the first time, I heard her breathing.

The feelings of fear and hope were impossible to differentiate. After placing a kiss on my forehead to soothe me, her beloved, Faith waited.

Nothing. No sound. Just dark silence.

> *Faith sat on the bench beside me. She had been close to me all my life, but that evening, for the first time, I heard her breathing.*

The decision had to be made. Would I enter this love story or leave? Would I remain a mere acquaintance of Faith, or would I open the door? Would I stay shielded and safe from her for the rest of my life, or would I risk the embrace? The story of the universe is a love story, and I was invited to enter.

I did. I said my first prayer.

"God."

Nothing more. Nothing more needed to be said.

I acknowledged far more than can fit into the word. I had entered a new reality, the one in which the mystery is part of being. With that one-word prayer, I acknowledged that I am not in charge of anything, really. I am not in charge of my own life, let alone the lives of others. I acknowledged that I am dependent on others and that others are dependent on me. I admitted that life is always greater than my own life, that there is no end to my ignorance and therefore to my knowing. Every thought I have, every feeling I experience, and every action I take is a participation in a life larger than mine.

Once I said my first prayer, once I used the word "God," I realized how inadequate, beaten, and broken this poor word really is. It does not mean anything, really. Any meaning we attach to it will sooner or later be found wanting. It is what we experience at the edge of that word that matters. It is about what we encounter once we break through the explanations.

My first prayer became a declaration of my presence in the community of the entire universe, from the weeds growing around that bench to celestial beings who might be there watching the scene. My prayer was my greeting to the larger world: "Hello, I am here. How is everybody doing?" A statement of gratitude: "Thank you for giving me this unearned right to live!" And an expression of hope: "The future is unknown!"

I walked back to the barracks without fully understanding anything of what I have just described. I just experienced it. Understanding came later. I felt moisture from the Beloved's lips still on my forehead, my heart and lungs pulsing in exhilaration, my hands embracing my own body, my eyes blinking through my tears, my face blushing under the stars. I wanted another kiss.

But that was it for the night.

A MYSTERY THAT CAN BE KNOWN

The prophet Isaiah wrote of God as someone we can't ever really know.

"'For my thoughts are not your thoughts, neither are your ways my ways,' declares the Lord. 'As the heavens are higher than the earth, so are my ways higher than your ways and my thoughts than your thoughts,'" says Isaiah.[1] From the beginning of creation, when darkness brooded over the earth, to impenetrable veils and clouds associated with the presence of God, to the mystery of salvation talked about in the New Testament, the Bible as a whole assumes the concealment of God. Even its last book, the book of Revelation, conceals far more than it reveals.

"Truly you are a God who hides himself," says the prophet.[2]

Most people are accustomed to thinking of religion as a journey to answers. I did. Too soon after my first passionate affair with God culminated in the covenant of baptism, the urge to control my experience of God led me to see religion as a way of taking control of my life. Mastery, structure, and power became important. I learned to admire evangelists who spoke about God with confidence. An evangelist (the one who brings *evangelion*, a Greek word meaning good news) would start a public event by taking cards from his pocket, each with a question that people had submitted the day before. He, always a man, would answer these questions with the confidence of someone who has mastered his subject. He then dished out the answers to the rest of us, who were hungry for certainty. The answers were followed by a sermon consisting of airtight arguments about the love of God and a heartwarming story to seal the deal.

> *"Something is missing here. Where is the struggle, where is the pain, where is the desire, where is the passion?"*

Back in the big city, after my service in the army was completed, I would take my old friends to evangelistic meetings full of hope for them. Thinking back, I wonder what I was expecting. Was I expecting my friends to say, "Wow, you really nailed God down. It is all so obvious! I want to have all the answers too!" Such responses rarely, if ever, came. One honest friend broke it to me: "Something is missing here. Where is the struggle, where is the pain, where is the desire, where is the passion? Your preachers are full of answers, but there is no wind of Spirit messing up their hair! How did you fall in love with *that*?" I didn't fall in love with *that*, I realized. I fell in love with the Beloved.

We religious people love to make God obvious. But God remains hidden.

Like a lover.

In a relationship with a lover, even if the relationship takes a lifetime—especially when it takes a lifetime—mystery is built into what is revealed. There comes a moment when the search for more and more data about the person we love is not just insufficient but misleading. What is hidden about a person is just as important as what is known, and only a relational experience can hold what is known and what is not known in harmony. Both knowing and not knowing become a part of revelation, a way love works.

Saint Thomas Aquinas wrote:

> *I said to God, "Let me love you."*
> *And He replied, "Which part?"*
> *"All of you, all of you," I said.*
> *"Dear," God spoke, "you are as a mouse wanting to*
>   *impregnate a tiger."*[3]

Religion scholar Karen Armstrong tells of an ancient Indian ritual that is instructive for those of us seeking answers. Two priests enter a contest. One of them attempts to define Brahman, the ultimate reality, in the form of a riddle. His opponent replies in kind, in an equally elusive and poetic way. The exchange continues until one of the two reduces the other to silence. In that silence, where there are no more words left to be spoken, Brahman is present.

Mystics from Jewish, Christian, and Muslim traditions teach us that God is someone whom we cannot even speak of and who must therefore be experienced in silence. That's why, for example, Muslims don't have religious trappings in their worship space. Just space. And people. Under God. That's why silence is one of the common responses to God in the Bible, embodied in the Quaker tradition of worship.

Words reveal, but they also obscure.

In words, we attempt to hold God. In silence, God holds us.

God is a mystery we cannot speak of.

Nevertheless, the prophet Isaiah continues, "as the rain and the snow come down from heaven, and do not return to it without watering the earth and making it bud and flourish, so that it yields seed for the sower and bread for the eater, so is my word that goes out from my mouth."[4] As the skies are far from earth, so is God. At the very same time, as rain and snow soak the earth, so does God. God is so different from us that we can never grasp God, and so close to us that we cannot avoid God.

In *How (Not) to Speak of God*, Peter Rollins captures this wisdom of the centuries succinctly: "That which we cannot speak of is the one thing about whom and to whom we must never stop speaking."[5] What if God, instead of being absent, is in reality hyperpresent, overwhelming both our experience and our language? What if God is a mystery to us precisely because God's presence is actually blinding us? What if mystery is built into the revelation of God, and the more revelation we have, the more mystery we experience? Rollins asks, what if instead of being limited by God's absence, we are short-circuited by the excess of God's presence?

> *What if God is a mystery to us precisely because God's presence is actually blinding us?*

That which we cannot speak of is the one thing about whom and to whom we must never stop speaking.

WHY NOT LOVE IT SO?

The prophet Isaiah goes on to describe the way creation responds to this divine saturation of the earth: "You will go out in joy and be led forth in peace; the mountains and hills will burst into song before you, and all the trees of the field will clap their hands."[6] For the prophet, this hyperpresence of God is not something we can perceive by mere intellect.

God's presence feels. Like music.

And music reveals. And hides.

Like all art, music hides an excess of meaning. When Jesus said about his teachings, "Those who have ears to hear, let them hear," he was not addressing the deaf but rather everyone standing around him.

Music seeks a response. An embrace. A dance.

According to the prophet, everyone and every thing—including the mountains, the hills, and the trees of the field—can hear the music and respond. Even when there is no nature, for those who hear the music, response of the world is still there. In the sprawling suburbs of Southern California, it was highways bursting into song before us; in New York's rush hour, it is subway doors clapping their hands. Once we hear the music, ranging from lament to joy, the world changes, and we dance. The moment we start breaking down the music into answers, we stop listening. And the moment we stop listening, we stop dancing. We force the meaning instead of surrendering to what

Christian scholar and mystic Eugene Peterson calls "unforced rhythms of grace."[7]

For the mystics of the ages, all orthodoxy, all law, all tradition, and all theology are, at the end of the day, inadequate for attaining oneness with God. Sufis—poets and mystics of Islam—bursting contemporary conceptual frameworks of religion, have held that even the Quran, which they respect as the direct speech of God, is still found wanting. They would insist, "Who reads love letters in the embrace of the Beloved?"

Religion is a shell. Love is the pearl inside.

My Sufi friend Rabia invited me to a mosque in downtown Manhattan where she worships every Thursday evening starting at seven. I left home telling my wife I would be back around nine. People began arriving at the mosque right at seven, sitting on the floor, circulating a basket filled with sweet dates and sugary delights, sipping tea, acknowledging each other's presence. A caring conversation followed, sweeter than the dates and delights. A man had a problem with his knee, a young woman was pregnant, someone lost a job, there was a guest in town. The group blessed each person, praying the first prayer of the Quran, known as "The Opening" (al-Fatiha), over and over again, once for each person mentioned. Listening to them, I remembered the voice of Sadika, my grandmother on my father's side, teaching me the same melodious words. She

> *Religion is a shell. Love is the*
> *pearl inside.*

would pray "*Bism Allah, el-Rahman, el-Rahim. Elhamdu lilAhi, Rab ela'alamin; El-Rahman, el-Rahim*..." And then one more time. And again...

About 7:45, the focus shifted seamlessly from caring for one another to enlightening and encouraging words spoken by the worship leader, then to chanting God's names, and then to moving one's body to act out the meaning of the words the people were saying. It all culminated in dervishes twirling, turning around their heart as an axis of life where, as the Quran says, great God dwells. They turned counterclockwise, the right part of the body closing in on the left, embracing their own human heart where God is. Left hand thrust upward toward the sky, enacting the reception of the love of God; right hand turned downward to bless the earth on which we live.

They took their time.

When I walked to the back of the mosque to retrieve my shoes from the pile, I looked at my watch and saw that it was after midnight! Where had the time gone? I rushed to call my wife with a revised time of arrival. She did not answer, and I left a message. Just as I was about to say goodbye and exit, one of the dervishes said, "Come upstairs for dinner."

"Dinner? Now?"

I had *had* dinner—six hours earlier. Why not call it breakfast?

The thought of eating and chatting this late on a weeknight was preposterous for a family person like me—irresponsible, really. I didn't know what to do, so I decided to stay. All the brothers and sisters, as they called one another, came upstairs and sat on the floor around low tables. While the city was asleep, here the great date with God went on! The plates were passed, conversations multiplied, and a happy cook came out with a large pot of lentil soup, fresh cheese, olives, and bread. It was all sprinkled with another five *al-Fatiha* prayers.

By the time we ate, it was one-thirty. In a moment of silence, I asked, "Do you people go to work tomorrow?"

"Mm-hmmm," they said, nodding, mouths full.

I laughed. This was ridiculous. They were teachers, service industry workers, artists, businesspeople, regular hardworking New Yorkers. They responded in kind, laughing with me.

How could they live like this?

Why would they live like this?

It was three in the morning when I quietly turned the key to my house, careful not to wake the children. Vesna, was asleep with her arm flung out, waiting for me. And right at that moment, a memory came rushing back to me. When she and I were dating more than twenty years ago, we lived fifty miles apart. In the middle of the week, one week after another, after my parents went to bed, I would sneak out of house, go to the bus station, take a slow bus ride through the night, walk to her apartment building, and wait for her to come out to surprise her early in the morning.

And for what? To see her for fifteen minutes on the way to her morning classes. To walk next to her. And perhaps steal a kiss. Then I would go back home on the bus, and my whole day would be ruined. And she never wondered why. She knew why. It made sense to her. And it made sense to me. We loved each other so.

> "What about this gift of life we will never fully understand? Why not love it so?"

I would tell her over and over again in different ways, like saying another al-Fatiha after another, "I love you."

Looking at her in the bed that night in New York and drawn to her embrace, I asked myself, "What about this gift of life we will never fully understand? Why not love it so?"

THE ECSTASY OF INCOMPLETENESS

Mystics held that the desire for God is sweeter than any knowledge of God. They would say that we are "nourished by our hunger" for God. The Christian apologist C. S. Lewis puts it succinctly in his book *Surprised by Joy* when recalling moments in his life when the joy of knowing God touched him, albeit fleetingly. He says that this joy, "sharply distinguished from both Happiness and from Pleasure" is "an unsatisfied desire which is itself more desirable than any other satisfaction!"[8]

Song of Songs, a book in the Hebrew Scriptures, uses sensual love between two lovers to describe the ecstasy of knowing and being known by God. "All night long on my bed I looked for the one my heart loves; I looked for him but did not find him.

I will get up now and go about the city, through its streets and squares; I will search for the one my heart loves."[9] In the sacred Scripture, sensuality permeates the text because of the limitation of our conceptual God talk.

Law could not touch God. Theology could not. Words could not.

So instead of collapsing God into a string of words or concepts, mystics stretched the language to describe their experience. Throughout history, they guarded a path to God in a climate of life-threatening fundamentalism, crossing the artificial boundaries between theology and poetry, thick walls between one religion and the other, apparent chasms between God and humanity.

Honoring the mystical experience of the Sabbath rooted in Judaism, Saint Thomas Aquinas wrote:

> *On the Sabbath try and make no noise that*
> *goes beyond your*
> *house.*
>
> *Cries of passion between lovers*
> *are exempt.*[10]

The Sufi poet Shams-ud-din Muhammad Hafiz wrote about Christ:

> *I am*
> *a hole in a flute*
> *that the Christ's breath moves through—*

listen to this

music.[11]

And about the sheer joy of daily life with God:

God

and I have become

like two giant fat people living

in a tiny

boat.

We

keep bumping into

each other

and

l

a

u

g

h

i

n

g.[12]

Tukaram, a seventeenth-century Indian poet, wrote about the futility of our God talk:

I think God gave us the wrong

medicine.

Let's take a poll: How enlightened have you been

feeling?

I bet He keeps a private stash

of something that

really

works.[13]

The Christian mystic Catherine of Sienna wrote about her sensual experience of God:

> *"I won't take no for an answer,"*
> *God began to say*
> *to me*
>
> *when He opened His arms each night*
> *wanting us to*
> *dance...*[14]

So did Saint Theresa of Avila:

> *When He touches me I clutch the sky's sheets,*
> *the way other*
> *lovers*
> *do*
>
> *the earth's weave*
> *of clay.*
>
> *Any real ecstasy is a sign*
> *you are moving*
> *In the right*
> *Direction,*
>
> *don't let any prude tell*
> *you otherwise.*[15]

In a relational world, mere information will not do. The moment we think we know someone is the moment we don't. Certainty about the other, whether human or divine, effectively does away with the relationship. To acknowledge the limitations of our faith language does not make God less but more. And it does not make our love more elusive but more real.

The moment we think we know someone is the moment we don't.

Without certainty, this world is a frightening place to live. We are fragile creatures who crave as much certainty in this life as we can possibly get. We lose jobs, health, lovers, and homes, and we know how exhausting uncertainty can be. But the anguish of uncertainty about God is also a source of tremendous comfort: while we do not grasp God, God grasps us.

It is a different kind of certainty. Our sense of incompleteness and our unfulfilled desire pull us from our reasoned private world into the universe as is, a place of freedom where the cosmic love story is unfolding. That's why religion and its words are for lovers, for people who want to live with burning passion and outrageous hope.

The same goes for what we think of as exclusively reasonable endeavors, such as science. Every discovery in a research lab is nothing but a stop on the journey of a lover. My friend Milorad Kojić, a genetic biologist from the Upper West Side here in Manhattan, is a hard-core scientist, one of those characters who, once in a lab, lose all sense of the outside world. To me, he is a mystic! And not because of his deeply intellectual, Eastern Orthodox–tinted Dostoyevskian magnetism but because his love is even greater than his great intellect. Even a scientist—a champion of reason—starts out with certainty and then, stepping into faith, challenges what has been proved. Every innovation begins with a transgression. The preponderance of data and people of knowledge may say one thing, but a true scientist, a lover of life—imagine the person dressed in a glorious white robe like a dervish—twirls in the research lab and sees what others cannot see, suffering through an intense unfulfilled desire, seeking truth and beauty concealed behind appearances. The scientist is mad, stepping into the unknown. Conversely, it is the certainty of a priest, the certainty of a politician, and the certainty of a scientist that hold the world back.

Uttering my first prayer was the most courageous act of my life because it was an act of surrendering to something greater than my own singular self and the sum of all I knew. I discovered that for most of us, surrender implies withdrawal, weakness, and passivity. When an enemy stronger than we are advances, we surrender. We pride ourselves on our ability to stand and defend rather than submit or yield. But the surrender of faith is a surrender to a lover, not to an enemy. When we take a step toward our lover, we take a step into a world where not knowing is a part of being. I prayed my first prayer because I sensed that refusing to surrender carries its own bondage. If I cannot in some way surrender to the unknown, I cannot love, and there is no greater bondage than the inability to love.

Now, a quarter century later, this single-word prayer—"God"—still works for me. I sense it when I need to say it, perhaps once a year, and I find a place where I am alone, and I say the word, and the world shifts from certainty to possibility, a common moment becomes eternal, here becomes everywhere, anything becomes part of everything, and a new way of seeing, experiencing, and even remembering opens up for me.

TRUE RELIGIOUS EXTREMISTS

There are clear and obvious disadvantages to the fact that we don't have the certainties that come with having all the answers about God. Yet with a God who cannot be mastered, we gain a significant advantage: no creature can act in the name of God.

A childhood friend who joined me in faith told me after four years of desperation about his inability to stay in love with God: "Sometimes I wish God would chain me to himself." Interestingly, the Hebrew Bible, New Testament, and Quran do not use such images to describe the human relationship with God. We are not imprisoned, restrained, or contained by God. Force is not an option.

With a God who cannot be mastered, we gain a significant advantage: no creature can act in the name of God.

But many people want chains. They are afraid they might leave God or God might leave them, and instead of pursuing a dynamic love relationship with God, they want to settle for static bondage to God. Their inner chains are made of imagined certainties created by their fears—belief systems that automatically exclude all other belief systems in direct proportion to how much the other belief systems differ from their own.

There is a wide spectrum of ways human beings idolize certainty about God. At one end of the spectrum—the less violent end—are people who are deeply concerned about the integrity of their religion, theology, practice, and tradition, so they act as the guardians of these things. They see their belief system as a symphony that needs to be reined in instead of played out, a complex but controllable piece of music that encompasses everything one can know about God. Instead of feeding their soul on the music itself, these religious conductors use a tremendous amount of energy and resources to *control* the orchestra of their belief and practice. Preoccupied and often exhausted by the God talk of their religion, they stop listening to the music. The Beloved wants to play and dance and kiss and caress, but they are too busy managing the orchestra and the score. All sloppiness, digression, flexibility, and challenge to the authority has to be rooted out! Every side note, every skipped beat, every unfinished movement, every unplanned sound, every new instrument, every improvised measure in one's life or the life of one's religious community rekindles a fear that the symphony will collapse into cacophony.

More problematic, though, at the other, more violent end of the spectrum of the idolatry of certainty about God, are those whose fear of doubt and uncertainty becomes a source of self-hatred. Dynamic and uncertain relationships with ourselves, other human beings, and God are too difficult for them to bear. Since God's revelation both reveals and conceals and since carrying trust and doubt intertwined in the fabric of life is threatening to them, they gravitate to acts they hope can resolve the uncertainty of faith. And destruction resolves.

Acts of violence become the way to push themselves from unbelief over the threshold of the paradox of faith and into the certainty and finality that comes with destruction. Death—for others and for themselves—is preferable to uncertainty. Because they cannot find peace with their creaturehood, they take upon themselves God's prerogative: to create or end life. These certainty worshipers do not grasp the fundamental religious teaching of the interdependence of all life. Destruction of others destroys oneself. Detached from the image of God in themselves, they act on their self-hatred.

Thus the people we call "religious extremists" are not extremely religious—or even religious at all. (I do not include here people pushed to the edges of physical, emotional, or cultural survival acting in extreme ways as a response to predatory practices of global markets.) On the contrary, they become what they despise. Their devotion is a mirror image of the devotion of a mindless consumer. To blow oneself up in order to obtain access to sighing virgins (or any other bliss, for that matter) expresses nothing but a lust for extreme goods and services—only in this case it's celestial goods and services instead of earthly ones—and a perception of God as a supplier.

> *In the embrace, it will not do to tell our lover that she or he is "great." We see our Beloved as "the greatest" and "the only," and that is what we say.*

In contrast, the symbolism and metaphoric language of religion offer an invitation to a love relationship with God, a relationship sustained by the unknown as well as the known. Religion asks us to enter a love story. With the Beloved, we can make natural, authentic, and, yes, absolute claims about God that can supply certainty for our tattered lives. Although our love affair with God cannot provide our heads with absolute knowledge of God, it does make absolute claim on our hearts. Our lives turn around, completely. So completely, in fact, that we have to resort to superlative language to speak about it. We talk about our Beloved as "only one" and as "full and final" because the ecstasy of the affair with the Beloved comes full blast, not in part. Our confessional love language is thus naturally and authentically superlative. It cannot be otherwise. In the embrace, it will not do to tell our lover that she or he is "great." We see our Beloved as "the greatest" and "the only," and that is what we say.[16]

But so-called religious extremists can't do this. They reject the deepest teachings of their religion about God, not because they have love for God, but because they *don't*. The real relationship with God has infinite nuances that are unbearable to them, so they have to devise a lesser god, a god that can be resolved with an act of destruction.

At their best, religions teach us how to love life in the midst of the uncertainty. People who destroy themselves or others in the name of their religion are actually people who don't know how to love and be loved. And that's why perhaps, paradoxically, there is nothing but love that can really stop them.

> *Religions teach us how to love life in the midst of the uncertainty.*

Why, then, I wonder, do we call them "religious extremists"? That implies they are religious heavyweights. So what does that make the people who courageously and humbly live with complexities and unanswered questions, who give their lives in service to their fellow human beings, who suffer injustice and even true martyrdom (suffering *imposed* on them), who challenge the culture of violence and find ways to change the world without destroying it? Religious lightweights?

Downplaying our religious histories, traditions, teachings, and practices only forfeits our opportunity to push back against the destructive force of the idolaters of certainty. Their conviction cannot be countered by nonconviction but only by a passion stronger than theirs—the passion of a lover.

THE FRATERNITY OF MILK

In studying developmental psychology in graduate school, I learned of an experiment that tried to determine infants' reactions to their mothers' voices. The researchers established a communication system with infants through highly sophisticated, electronically outfitted nipples that could measure the intensity of an infant's sucking—supernipples, if you will. They would expose each infant to a mix of recorded women's voices, only one of them being the infant's mother's voice. In the first part of the experiment, they connected each supernipple to an amplifier and made the mother's voice stand out from others in proportion to the intensity of the infant's sucking. In the second part of the experiment, the researches reversed the reaction: the stronger the infant sucked, the quieter the mother's voice would become in relation to the other female voices. Astonishingly, they found that each newborn would suck more or suck less, as necessary, in order to hear its mother's voice more clearly.

I found this not only a fascinating scientific finding but also a spiritual one. Muhammad Ibn 'Arabî, a thirteenth-century Arab Muslim, author of more than 350 works—perhaps the greatest mystic philosopher of Islam alongside Jalaluddin Rumi—and a towering figure in human spirituality, writes in his most comprehensive work, *Meccan Illuminations*, about three kinds of communities: the Brotherhood of Blood (an exclusive family of consanguinity and kinship), the Brotherhood of Water (a wider community of the people who believe the same thing, our coreligionists), and the Brotherhood of Milk (a community across all human boundaries connected through their suckling at the breast of Divine Love).[17]

This strikes a deep chord in my own life. My family, I thought, was restricted to my blood relatives, people I found myself with in this world. When I was baptized by immersion in the water, my community expanded. Water has been a common way of declaring one's embrace of a specific spiritual path and the community that takes it. Now, two decades later, I want to belong to this Fraternity of Milk, a community that is bent on suckling for the sweet knowledge of the Giver of Life, across all human boundaries, all in their own place and in their own way.

In his epistle, John, perhaps the first mystic of the Christian church and author of the fourth gospel, wrote about God in a particularly unusual manner. Instead of mincing his words about God by using negatives, comparison, contrast, metaphors, and other linguistic devices allowing a guarded approach to the concept of God, John made a passionate attempt at direct statements about who God is.

"Dear friends," he writes, "let us love one another, for love comes from God. Everyone who loves has been born of God and knows God. Whoever does not love does not know God, because God is love.... God is love. Whoever lives in love lives in God, and God [lives] in him."[18] John identifies God as love, locates God in everyone who loves, and locates everyone who loves in God. Here, sensing the tendencies of a newborn religion to pose as the sole custodian of God in the world, while insisting that God "showed his love *among us*" by sending Jesus to us, John breaks out of the Christian confines of the word "God" and relates the reality behind it to all humanity. Not every human being is my blood sibling and only some human beings can be my water siblings, but surely, every human being *can* be my milk sibling.

God is our lover and therefore never to be mastered. Interpreting revelation solely as something that makes God knowable narrows our consciousness, dulls our emotions, and lessens our understanding.

Interpreting revelation solely as something that makes God knowable narrows our consciousness, dulls our emotions, and lessens our understanding.

Our situation of "knowing God" is thus similar to that of a baby being held by its mother.[19] In her hands, the baby does not "understand" the mother but rather experiences being known by the mother. In the same way, the revelation of God we have received from God is not just coming from the words of our Scriptures but also through this gift of life that holds us. Life itself is a revelation, a site where God sustains and transforms us. We are unable to grasp God, even as we are being transformed by God's grasp. In this act of holding us, God is like a mother, revealed in a way that is real but remains a secret.

Mira, a woman poet in sixteenth-century India acclaimed by Hindus, Christians, and Muslims, wrote:

God has
a special interest in women
for they can lift this world to their breast
and help Him
comfort.[20]

The story of the universe is a love story. Held by our mother when we are young, held by our lover when we are adults, held by our child when we are old—whenever we are held, by a nurse, friend, or a kind stranger, we experience this story of the universe.

Sitting on a bench away from the army barracks between two worlds, my desire for certainty was not fulfilled. I left desiring another kiss. And that's why I remain a believer! My unfulfilled yearning for God is sweeter than any other desire ever fulfilled. My uncertainty with God is more comforting than any certainty I have ever known.

I am held.

And the kisses of the Beloved keep coming.

5

WHERE DOES YOUR HEART GO?

BENEATH THE SMOLDERING SMOKE HOVERING over Manhattan after the September 11 attacks, we were busy writing letters, typing e-mails, and making phone calls to people around the world, asking for money and spending it before we ever received it. Hundreds of professional counselors, relief workers, and helpful or curious out-of-town folks came through our old church building. Up to fifty at a time slept in the basement in sleeping bags on an embarrassingly dirty carpet, visited by mice, with no showers or other amenities of home. Upper East Side neighborhood businesses found out about our work and offered to sponsor the meals. Mary Erra, a can-do Manhattanite who lived in one of those doorman-attended high-rise apartment buildings off Park Avenue came to a support group my wife and I helped facilitate, and offered to help. In a matter of hours, she plastered every floor of her building with flyers asking residents to "donate a shower." Soon there was a steady stream of people from our church basement entering the life space of strangers, using their nice bathrooms, eating warm meals prepared by their hands, stopping at the living room windows to take in million-dollar views over the Manhattan skyline, receiving this moment of respite as a gift.

New York was a seven-layer salad that the tragedy tossed. The layers mixed and people entered each other's worlds. At times, I would stand aside and watch in quiet, dazed, disbelief at an apparent miracle—complete strangers eating at these hosts' kitchen tables, their hair still wet and their bodies still tingly from a hot shower, their hosts watching them with worried smiles. I couldn't remember seeing anything that hopeful ever before.

> *New York was a seven-layer salad that the tragedy tossed. The layers mixed, and people entered each other's worlds.*

After the attacks on the World Trade Center and the anthrax scare just weeks later, otherwise fearless New Yorkers began to show cracks in their composure. While many of us were busy healing the rift with Muslim people that was opening fast in our collective traumatized psyche, others were busy finding fault with all things Islamic, and with us, their empathizers. They questioned our loyalty to America, to Christianity, to reason, to justice, to homeland security, and even to New York City. For me, it was a case of déjà vu. In those days after 9/11, the fearful faces from times past in my home country, Yugoslavia, kept coming back to me in conversations and dreams. I would have nightmares of being asked to fight and then getting lost behind enemy lines. The drums of Serbian and Croatian patriotism were beating through the media with resonance feeding off and amplifying one another.

And now the same thing was happening in this global "clash of fundamentalisms." We soon realized that people's borderline hysterical fear of Muslims, a newfound *other* in their midst, was depleting our energy and dragging down our relief efforts. Two thoughtful and courageous women, Iowaka Barber and Sylvia Hordosch from our church community, suggested that we organize a public meeting to create an opportunity for Muslim leaders to share the treasures of their faith, practice, and culture. We invited two prominent imams in Manhattan, a woman from the organization Muslims Against Terrorism, and a Christian public health professional and activist who had lived for many years in Islamic countries and could provide his unique perspective.

I communicated the idea to everyone I came across and found, to my chagrin, some people strangely unmoved. Within hours, several well-meaning concerned neighbors advised me not to hold the event. They predicted trouble. "This is only encouraging the terrorists. If Muslims don't like America, they can go and live over there," pointing the way with a flick of the hand.

I had to make a decision whether to hold the event or not, but I was exhausted and unsure. My congregation suffered in a particularly difficult way. Michael Baksh, the new chairman of our church board, was a handsome, professional, and kind young man from Pakistan, "a gentleman of the Kingdom of God," as we affectionately called him. On his first day at work in the World Trade Center, the first airplane flew directly into Michael's office on the ninety-fourth floor. We waited, week after week, comforting the family and calling on God to heed our prayers and bring Michael back alive. I had a dream of his being stuck in a subway two city blocks from the crater and emerging from one of the shafts on the street, saying, "Whew, that was close!" Every weekend, our whole congregation, including Michael's wife, Christina, and their two little children, came to pray. We would stand in a circle, and one of our leaders, Dan Fahrbach, would pray, "God, can a prayer change anything? If it can, we vote for life." Christina and I went to the large hall of an old armory set up by the city where family survivors and their clergy could turn in items like toothbrushes or combs on which traces of the DNA of the missing loved one might be found, in the distant hope of confirming the identities of remains as they were recovered. We wanted to know Michael's fate. But hope eventually gave way to exhaustion.

> *Instead of helping us imagine our life together, the government, prodded by media hungry for news, led the nation to believe that the world was like one enormous ultimate fighting octagon ring.*

I was tired of hope, and fear began to creep in.

In the depths of our collective sorrow, Americans had difficulty imagining living peacefully with "those people," tarring all Muslims with a broad brush. And instead of helping us imagine our life together, the government, prodded by media hungry for news, led the nation to believe that the world was like one enormous ultimate fighting octagon ring. Demonstrations of power were paramount, the first and indispensable step to assuage our grief and regain our footing.

And I discovered that to many Americans, I was still one of "those people." One man confronted me over a seemingly irrelevant snippet of information: my name. "One of the hijackers was named Samir," he pointed out and paused, his eyes boring into mine. "Isn't your name Samir?" I like to think he was only following the government's admonition to "be vigilant," but this encounter made me further question the wisdom of holding the event I had been organizing. I decided to call my family in Croatia.

"Cancel the event and shut up," my dad said confidently over the phone. He argued that Americans didn't have a recent memory of being collectively hurt. When faced with loss, he told me, they would likely respond with rage rather than grieving. My sister, Bisera, chimed in, saying that Americans had been on vacation from history and now the vacation was over. They now had to join the world, and, she insisted, I was not the one to invite them. My family was convinced that Americans didn't know how to cope with loss of control and would probably resort to hurting others in their efforts to recover their sense of self-respect.

"But Dad," I pleaded, "the Islam we know is radically pacifist. That's what I grew up with. In Yugoslavia, I never saw Muslims engaged in any violence whatsoever. We know that to kill a human being is to betray Islam. We cannot create life, and we therefore cannot take it. Why should I be afraid to talk about this?"

> "We know that to kill a human being is to betray Islam. We cannot create life, and we therefore cannot take it."

"People whose pride has been hurt see warmongering as patriotism. They *need* an enemy. And peacemakers are a convenient target!" my dad said, calling on his substantial experience from the Balkans and wearing down any remnants of my hopefulness. I should, the family advised, zip my mouth shut, lie low, and not put myself out there as a target.

I put the phone down and cried.

I get upset when anyone says things like "God did that," "God wants this," or "God told me so." How can anyone really know? But strangely, the more that people from the neighborhood spoke against the event, the more the warnings of my family seemed to make sense, the more I learned about unsuspecting people with Arab names like mine being abducted by bewildered government authorities, the more sure I became that God wanted this event to happen!

And that was another déjà vu. I remembered I had experienced the same kind of pressure to conform years before, when my Muslim family and secular friends descended on me with full force, begging me to reverse my decision to become a Christian.

Following a still, small voice speaking from within, I rejected their demands. Now, in the aftermath of 9/11, I realized again that it was not stubbornness that compelled me to reject the warnings of concerned New Yorkers and my family back in Croatia. It was the same small inner voice. This defiance against the other voices in my life was not a fantasy of self-importance or a delusional religious experience. The voice was like a pilot light that Someone or Something had lit, and instead of snuffing it out, my tears just fed the flame.

I tried not to listen to the voice, but the fire burned, burned, burned. And eventually it empowered me. We went ahead with the event. The church was filled, New York music professionals from the neighborhood volunteered with their art, wise people spoke, angry people spoke, sad people spoke, everyone listened, and our hope was restored!

> *I made one resolution for the rest of my life: I am going to risk more and sooner.*

We realized we were humans first, and followers of our religions and ideologies second, which in turn served our religions better than having it the other way around. Standing a couple of city blocks from the debris where the towers used to be I made one resolution for the rest of my life: I am going to risk more and sooner.

A year of hard and productive work followed. We grieved together, labored together, prayed together, sang together. Oh, we loved each other so well! On the first anniversary of the attacks, tens of thousands of New Yorkers gathered for a free concert in Central Park. When Billy Joel finished singing "New York State of Mind," we all exhaled, as if for the first time after the attacks. The voice of my friend Derek Lynton, a lawyer from the Bronx and another "gentleman of the Kingdom of God," broke the silence. "It has been September 11 for a whole year. Tomorrow, finally, for the first time, it will be September 12."

Ever since, I have been asking, where does that small voice inside of us come from? The voice speaks no words but is real nonetheless, empowering and clear. It does not come from religion, reason, or pragmatic considerations or even from a desire for self-preservation.

There are times in our lives, however rare, when we are called to stand against the entire world, against all other voices, and heed that small voice within.

But to what or whom are we listening when we hear it?

FIVE MINUTES BEFORE WE FALL ASLEEP

From the time I first heard the word "spirituality" in middle school, I felt drawn to the Eastern tradition of meditation. The Communist ideologues did not frown on the Eastern religions as they did on the monotheistic religions. Because Eastern religions were more concerned with "what is real" and less with "what is right and wrong," they thought small groups of Buddhists or Hindus posed no serious threat to the authorities and powers of the regime. For years, I had a notebook in which I diligently recorded my breathing routines, meditational practices, and astral projection exercises (also known as lucid dreams).

I learned that every day ends with five minutes of truth. Five minutes before we fall asleep, provided we are not exhausted, our minds are free to go anywhere because they don't have to go somewhere in particular. That's one of the moments during the day when thoughts are free to simply happen as they will. After all conscious thinking is done, we pull in the oars and our minds drift.

Where do they go? What safe harbor do our hearts yearn for in which to spend the night?

> *Observing our own inner life from the outside is not a skill that comes easily to just anyone.*

This is a hard question to answer because as soon as we become aware of our inner monologues, our self-comforting, our analyses, our rehearsals, or any other form of thinking, we start taking conscious control, and a controlled mind can't roam freely. Observing our own inner life from the outside is not a skill that comes easily to just anyone. Eastern practices of meditation have been exploring this for centuries, helping people step out of the flow of their thinking to observe their own thoughts—like King David in the Hebrew Scripture, who in the Psalms addressed his own thoughts, speaking to his own soul.

Fortunately, to fall asleep, we must let go. In our beds, we enter a zone of trust. We have to. As we say farewell to the conscious reality in which we are the masters of our individual domains, we enter a period of time when we cannot control our own selves, let alone the world. We leave everything in hands other than our own. We relinquish control. We release the clutch. We believe that in the not-too-distant future, we will wake up able to walk, talk, think, and feel all over again. We trust.

Trust in what?

If someone could record those five minutes of truth every night, the unvarnished stories of our lives would emerge, with characters, conflicts, and plots other than those we tell others and ourselves. What are the stories I tell myself, powers I run to when in danger, sources of value and meaning that I trust?

This question can't be answered by a person who is either awake or asleep. When we sleep, we trust something, but what we trust remains unspoken and unidentified, buried in the silence of the night. While awake, on the other hand, we trust the very same thing but what we trust remains equally hidden, unheard, masked by the noise of our thoughts. When asked the question "What do you believe in?" most of us are simply not capable of answering it accurately. Instead of identifying what we believe in, we identify what we want to believe in or what we think we should believe in or what we think others want us to believe in.

We have to be in between. Neither awake nor asleep. During these five minutes of truth, we think our thoughts are drifting away. But they are not drifting away. As we let go of them, they actually seek that place, that time, that reality, that worry, that treasure, that harbor. They go to our true god and an altar inside with a little flame burning on it. In the language of the ancient Scripture, everyone—whether religious or not—assigns ultimate worth to *something*. Everyone's heart goes somewhere. Everyone worships.

WHY RELIGIOUS AND NONRELIGIOUS PEOPLE ARE THE SAME

I realized that everyone worships something when I first came to New York to pastor a church in 1997. I got run over—not by a cab but by a thick cloud of dreams. It was as if a whole century's worth of the ambitions of New Yorkers had accumulated over time and now lingered in the air, this thick cloud of dreams filling the streets, never to be blown out of the city, every generation adding to its weight and size.

What if people who see themselves primarily as "religious" and those who see themselves primarily as "nonreligious" both do this for the same reason: to simplify and manage the otherwise unbearable complexity of human experience?

One can see these dreams in the architecture. Whatever we worshiped, we erected a temple for it. Throughout history, our tallest buildings have housed the objects of our devotion. In the past, the tallest buildings in the cities were religious buildings. That's where the highest powers, the most cherished values, and the deepest meanings were experienced. That's where the gods dwelled.

Serving as the custodian of the arts, entertainment, business, and banking, a haven for religious expressions of every stripe, and a stage for world politics, New York City is the dream capital of the planet and a city of shrines. When it lost its two towers, we felt as if our collective had lost its two front teeth.

A lot of energy has been spent arguing about religion. Religion is good; religion is bad. Polemicists trying to decide whether we are better off with or without religion have been cycling their ideas through popular magazines, radio and television, and best-selling books. But the discussion is losing steam because we are becoming exhausted with the artificial dichotomy we have assumed. Most of the polarizing contributors to these parallel monologues function under the assumption that to be religious or nonreligious is somehow fundamentally different. Is it really?

What if this difference, although real, is not nearly as significant as we assume? What if people who see themselves primarily as "religious" and those who see themselves primarily as "nonreligious" both do this for the same reason: to simplify and manage the otherwise unbearable complexity of human experience?

We all settle on something. We are all looking for something to unify our consciousness and order our experience. Even people who don't want to rest their hearts on anything offered by traditional religions are in fact resting their hearts on something. People who don't want to make any decision about the origin and nature of our reality, people who don't want to make any choices that would take them on a path of belief into anything definite for the rest of their lives, people who always want to "keep their options open"—they all make life choices.

If one doesn't make any choices that close off other options, one is really choosing not to make any choices that really matter, for choices that matter rule out the alternatives.[1] Take marriage, for example. One cannot mine the treasures of another person without making the choice of staying in the relationship. To migrate from one person to another, from one place to another, from one idea to another, thus keeping one's options open, is itself a choice.

> *If one doesn't make any choices that close off other options, one is really choosing not to make any choices that really matter.*

To adopt this nomadic self is like digging a well three feet deep in ten different places. This drive for freedom becomes a life of bondage to shallowness, freely making choices that don't matter. Not to make a choice about what matters and what we want to do with our lives is itself a choice, whether you are religious or not. Not to choose your path means you choose to be carried by whoever or whatever force comes along, like a raft on the open sea, buffeted by random waves and currents.

We all have one life, one world, one shot. Once this reality of having just this one chance is grasped, where we choose to stir our heart becomes paramount. A thing? A cause? An achievement? A feeling? A person?

A nongod is anyone or anything other than God. For the purpose of our discussion, God can be thought of as the substance behind the undeniable and undeconstructible wonder of life that sweeps over us all. If this definition of God sounds terribly imprecise, it is intentional. I offer it only for the purpose of contrasting God and nongods. A nongod would then be anything other than that, anything other than the source and sustenance of the eternal kind of life.

And that's where religious and nonreligious people are the same. On one hand, nonreligious people worship nongods such as work, possessions, spouses, lovers, children, family backgrounds, causes, looks, wits, education, political parties, nations, or anything under the sun that can free them from the task of relating their life to the whole. On the other hand, religious people who worship nongods such as church, doctrines, festivals, rituals, liturgy, laws, habits, or any other religious entity also avoid relating their lives to the whole. Either way, their hearts have latched onto an object.

Either way, the whole being begins to shrink. God—an utterly inadequate word to convey what it stands for—can never be an object we can name. God can only be a subject in whose presence or in whom we live. The altar we have in our hearts and the little flame burning on it can be an altar to God or to a nongod, regardless of whether one is religious or not. Nongods such as faith or reason relegate the discussion about what matters to narrow or specialized language such as salvation or heaven and to unproductive questions such as whether God exists (more about that in Chapter Seven, "The Blessing of Atheism").

In the Hebrew Bible, one reads about nations, tribes, families, and individuals having something to trust. Often their trust was placed in statuettes made of wood, stone, or clay that embodied all that they regarded as safe, certain, and life-giving. The Hebrew Scriptures called them idols. Today, life has no less uncertainty, and although we don't rely on statuettes to make the mystery manageable, we too have idols, as small and as fragile as those in ancient times:

"I have to please my parents."

"I have to please my priest."

"I have to discredit the person who makes me look incompetent."

"I have to discredit the people who disagree with my beliefs."

"I have to make a lot of money to feel safe."

"I have to do many good deeds to be loved by God."

"If this person does not love me, nobody will."

"If this religious community does not accept me, nobody will."

"If I don't get this job, I am a failure."

"If I don't achieve this status in my church or synagogue, I am a failure."

When cherished as the ultimate source of value and power in our life, our idols begin to have a life of their own, unifying our consciousness around them, shaping our assumptions, spinning out entire self-justifying belief systems, creating their own laws and definitions of success and failure. Eventually, they choke our lives with such narrow but all-important singular concerns.

While other people's idols may strike us as ridiculous, our own idols make a lot of sense to us. Nongods create delusional fields around us. We start to reason, feel, and behave in ways that can protect and justify the central position of our idols in our lives. The apostle Paul, the most prominent writer of the New Testament, says that the tragedy of a life lived for a nongod is a form of slavery. Whenever we worship an idol, Paul argues, one of two things happens. The first is that we may crush our idol by placing impossible expectations on it. When I expect my work to be my ultimate delight, I will ruin my health and relationships in order to succeed, which will in turn ruin my work. When I expect my child's success to validate me or when I expect my spouse to give me value as a person, these expectations burden my loved ones and ultimately crush them and destroy my family. Nothing and nobody can bear the weight of expectation to perform God's role in our lives.

> *While other people's idols may strike us as ridiculous, our own idols make a lot of sense to us.*

Alternatively, if we don't crush our idols, they will crush us.[2] They become our functional masters, and we serve them and obey them because we believe we must have them in order to live. To sustain our devotion to nongods, we invest more and more in them, but the more we give, the more they demand. We can never have enough of something we want that cannot give us what we need.

The same is true of religion.

THE IDOLATRY OF RELIGION

For many of us religious people, the supremacy of our chosen faith has become a nonnegotiable aspect of our religion. And when something other than God becomes a nonnegotiable value, an idol is established.

Judaism is not God. Christianity is not God. Islam is not God.

And anything that is not God, any nongod, can be an idol. Judaism, Christianity, and Islam can therefore be idols. Even at their very best, because even at their very best, they are still not God.

I became a Christian by—among other things—reading the works of the Danish existential philosopher Søren Kierkegaard. He argued that the moment one decides to become a Christian, one is susceptible to idolatry. He managed to criticize Christianity harshly and thoroughly, which, paradoxically, compelled me to become a Christian. It made me run to God.

To run to God is as much an exercise of running away from religion as it is one of running toward religion.

If God will always be more than any of the notions we have about God, is it possible to use "God in name" to justify attitudes, actions, rituals, and ethics that circumvent "God in substance"? The two are not the same. We can use God in name to betray God in substance. I have seen it in my Muslim family, in my Christian church family, virtually everywhere I turn. I've seen God used to force a person into a marriage

> *Our understanding of God is vital to us, but only if we recognize that our understanding of God is not God.*

("*God* wants us to be together"), to justify bad parenting ("I don't have time for you because I serve *God*"), to market products ("Spread the word about *God* by buying our T-shirts and bumper stickers"), to justify wars and destruction ("We are called to defend *God's* honor!")—on and on, opportunities abounding. Our understanding of God is vital to us, but only if we recognize that our understanding of God is not God, not God as God is.

Meister Eckhart's often-quoted prayer should stay with us for the rest of our religious days: "God rid me of God."

Although in the Bible, encounters with God are possible and our talk about God can be meaningful, the Bible also insists that we can never master God's essence or encompass God's being. Any attempt at that would render God not sovereign and our God-encounters and God-talk idolatrous.

Hinduism, by contrast, has opted for a different understanding of the word "idol" (*murti*, meaning "form"). Hindus embrace numerous idols as myriad aspects of a single reality so that none of them individually can be exhaustive or limiting of the whole.

That's why Hindus insist we must put "neti, neti" (meaning "not this, not that") before we say anything about the Divine. Forms are thus only multiple windows into one reality. That's also why Buddhism does not even deal with the notion of God and gods and opts instead for "ultimate reality," thus removing the temptation to abuse or even use the notion of God for any purpose whatsoever. Zen Buddhists are ready even to burn all Scriptures and kill the Buddha in order not to get caught up. For Hindus and Buddhists, the human concept of God is useful only because it is necessary. This "wisdom of humility" is not to be dismissed by monotheists who base their faith on a specific story of God's actions and revelation to humanity. We have all seen it over and over again: whenever a creature claims to have an exclusive grasp of God, someone gets hurt. That's the case even if God is described as pure grace, nothing but love, or Christ crucified, as is the case with the treasured teachings of Christianity. The reformer John Calvin himself said that "the human heart is an idol-making factory."

We have all been idolaters of our religions. We have all used God to acquire land, power, and influence and called it devotion.

SAVING OUR RELIGIONS

When we feel emptiness in our lives, when the pregnant void that fills our existence presses on us, we rush to speak of God. Forgetting that our speaking of God is never actually speaking of God but only of our understanding of God, we hastily fill the void with religion. What if, instead of casting ourselves as people who can explain God to others, we viewed our lives as a void into which God speaks? There is no wisdom without humility, without cultivating an empty space where we can learn instead of teach, receive instead of give, submit instead of control, lose instead of win.

> *What if, instead of casting ourselves as people who can explain God to others, we viewed our lives as a void into which God speaks?*

Because religion is the way we approach the mystery behind life and deal with the uncertainties of the human experience, relinquishing one's religion as the center of one's life is an excruciating experience. And that's why we need to be reminded again and again that religion is not the pearl but the shell that holds the pearl.

The way forward, then, is for our religion to become less.

And therefore more.

When we free our religion from the burden of being our God, we empower it. It begins to serve us and the world around us.

Religions that will matter in the future will enable their adherents to live in tension with their own religiosity, saying, "My religion is a witness to the pearl and a community built around it—never the pearl itself." In Christian terms, to hold one's religion lightly would be the strongest possible move into the reality of the Kingdom of God that Jesus invited people to. The founders of our religions rarely, if ever, defended religion. They were about something more.

Still, without religion, nothing we have learned about the eternal kind of life would be passed from generation to generation. Think of the wheel, fire, and writing, and imagine every new generation taking up the task of inventing them all over again. Every religion has a treasury of stories of victory and failure, glory and shame, directions for tried paths that lead to life and paths that lead to death, communities that have learned to let go of the bad and preserve what was worth preserving. Without religion, we would all be left drifting with our own meanings, isolated from one another, from our past, and from our future.

Many of us say, "I love spirituality, but I hate religion." This distinction is as attractive as it is difficult to maintain. Spirituality without religion can be frighteningly undemanding. To change the world, one must change oneself, and a person who is not willing to heed the spirituality of others—in other words, religion—can hardly hope to change. Can we really say, "I love knowledge, but I hate education?" Isn't education there to make us hungry for knowledge? Isn't religion there to make us hungry for the eternal kind of life?

BETTER THAN LIFE

To worship a nongod is to experience a narrowing of consciousness, whether that nongod is a car, a job, family, Judaism, Christianity, Islam, any religion, any cause, any bad or good thing—anything at all. To worship God, on the other hand, is a venture into reality, a disciplined exit from the delusional fields created around our idols, a constant pull toward the margins of what we know. The worship of God is about awareness, about mindfulness, about reverence for the gift of life, about regaining perspective, beyond self-expression, beyond our beloved religions. By worshiping God, we turn our sights farther, rescued from a preoccupation with ourselves and with our own life.

Religion at its best does not satisfy us but aggravates the sense of the absence of God and thus increases our longing. King David observed his own heart and cried out, "Oh God, you are my God, earnestly I seek you; my soul thirsts for you, my body longs for you, in a dry and weary land where there is no water."[3] The worship of God begins with the sense of our Beloved's absence. The psalmist calls God "my God" and in the same breath grieves over the absence of the God he calls "my." God is already "his," and that's why he feels the absence. All of our praise begins with dissatisfaction, and the dissatisfaction itself is a sign of God's presence, for we would never long for God if it were not for God's presence.

Which means that we will desire more of God than our religion can ever contain.

Two verses later, David sings as the Sufis would sing, "Your love is better than life!"[4]

> *Religion at its best does not satisfy us but aggravates the sense of the absence of God and thus increases our longing.*

This is one of those extreme statements of Scripture that, once heard, will not let you remain indifferent. Its pressure on our accustomed ways of thinking increases until our minds either expel the thought or adjust everything else to it. How can God be better than being alive? What this statement implies is that even our own life can be a nongod we worship. To merely live, even with life at its most fulfilling and fruitful, is still not worth living for! Only love is worth living for. Jesus, for example, believed, lived, and at the end enacted this truth on the cross: love is better than life.

> *That's what happens with nongods. You put your whole life on the line for them, and when you arrive, they amount to nothing more than a busload of tourists admiring your heroic effort.*

Robert, a childhood friend of mine from Germany, got into rock climbing. For many months, he practiced hard, bought the gear, and mastered the lingo. Then the time came for a weeklong trip culminating in a climb from dawn to dusk on a tall rock wall on a mountain peak. Afterward, he reported passionately, "I wanted to get to the top so badly, to get to that untouched place and look over the valley below!" No effort was too much.

He made it that day. He arrived at the top. I wondered how it must have felt to arrive. He continued, "I put my right hand over the brink, then my left, then I pulled myself to the top, and as I lifted my head, I saw it! Right in front of me. A bus! It was unloading Japanese tourists taking pictures of me, with big kind smiles, nodding their heads, then packing into the bus and leaving."

That's what happens with nongods. You put your whole life on the line for them, and when you arrive, they amount to nothing more than a busload of tourists admiring your heroic effort.

Wouldn't it be better to climb to a place that is "better than life"? And wouldn't that climb, even if unfinished, be sweeter than any other climb that is finished?

Believing in God saves us from believing in nongods. That's why atheism is inherent in Christianity, a kind of atheism that questions all our views of God and all our allegiance to religion. (This idea will be further developed in Chapter Seven.)

And that's one of the reasons we need religions other than our own.

Other religions can challenge (or at least help us see) the idols we create because they expand the whole territory of knowing. They pose difficult questions we don't want to ask, make assumptions we don't want to acknowledge or examine, create meaningful arguments against us we don't want to consider, and expose harmful practices we don't want to stop. Where we have created a vacuum of knowledge and virtue through our own religions, God enters that space through the religions of others—through strangers. When we let them come close and embrace them as our neighbors, they can help us see God's presence, grace, and care where we cannot see it on our own.

This mutual blessing can happen if God becomes more to us than our religion. Those who love God more than their religion will be able to learn without end, and as continual learners they can be safe teachers for others, offering their own precious perspectives and opening whole new vistas into life.

CONVERSION AND CONVERSION

Conversion is a not a process of generating faith in God but a process of transferring faith (that we already and always have) from nongods to God. When we withhold our ultimate devotion from nongods, we abandon a currency by which we have been measuring life for an entirely different currency. That's why we use the term "conversion."

Because religion is a nongod, converting from a religion to God is really not that different from converting from any other worldview to God.

Those of us who came to faith in God as outsiders to organized religion have at times been told by believers who grew up in a religion, "You are lucky. You have come from the outside and had an experience of conversion. Your difficult journey has actually been a blessing to you." Indeed, although this kind of conversion has been disruptive of our relationships, our life goals, our feelings, everything we think our lives ought to have, at the very same time the experience was life-giving.

However, for those who have grown up in a religion, the process of turning to God is equally hard and equally life-giving. If the prospect of transitioning your heart from your religion to the Kingdom of God makes you afraid, it is for a good reason. To do this *will* be disruptive of your relationships too, of your life goals, of your feelings, of everything you think your life ought to have. The emotional, social, financial, and every other cost is considerable.

But the sky is not falling. In fact, it is opening.

What if the religion to which you belong is just one of the cultures and structures that needs to be loved and supported but also resisted and challenged in favor of the Kingdom of God? If that is so, the transition from loyalty to your religious culture to loyalty to the Kingdom of God is every bit as glorious as coming from a "nonreligious" culture into the Kingdom of God. They are both conversions! It takes every bit as much faith and courage to step into it. Your way of life, your community, and even your own heart will suffer through an experience of displacing your religion from the center of your heart. And God will enter.

Here is my heartfelt invitation to take that step.

What I think is holding most of my friends back from becoming followers of God is not whether God exists, for our notion of existence is restricted. And it is not the mystery of everything we believe that is holding them, for people sense that beliefs are only our limited takes on reality. What holds them back is the refusal of religious people to see, admit, and resist the idolatry of their own selves in the form of their own religion. For that is what all idols are in the end: the worship of self.

And people who sense the vastness of life, the sheer grace of existence, the freedom to doubt and be different, the life-giving call to love our world, look at religion as we have it today and say, "Naah. Life with God should be more generous than that."

And they are right, right?

I suggest you take a deep breath now and join me for an exercise.

Let your religion go.

There is no reason to be afraid.

Breathe out.

Good...

Notice that nothing has changed as far as God is concerned. God is still the one in whom you are and breathe and have your being. Torah is still your guide for life. Jesus Christ is still your Lord and Savior. The Prophet Muhammad (peace be upon him) is still the Messenger.

Perhaps more so.

Already, now, God is beginning to enter the spaces that have been freed.

As you lie on your bed tonight, may your heart, released from the clutches of nongods, find rest in love that is better than life.

6

YOUR GOD IS TOO BIG

MY PARENTS RAISED ME TO SUCCEED. Before I took up my journey with God, I wanted to be someone important. I wanted to have a great education, a great house, a great car, a great wife, and great children—the great things in life that everyone wants. Still, the signals I got from family and society to want all these things paled in comparison to my secret ambition. I wanted way more. *I* wanted to be great.

Once I became a Christian, these fantasies of grandiosity were swept away by the teachings and life of Jesus.

Until I became a pastor. Like many of us at the time who watched the success of large church preachers, I wanted to be like them. I wanted a large building with a large budget. I dreamed of the time when people would buy recordings of my sermons, read my books, laugh at my jokes, and seek my advice. Of course, I was not aware of this at the time. None of us were. We were marching down the path of serving God!

My pre-Christian fantasies had not gone away. They had just been baptized with me. My dreams of grandiosity had been "sanctified" and refashioned into something far more difficult to see. And although this development was squarely a consequence of my own choices, I do blame the church—especially its contemporary Western version—for discipling so many of us down this path.

Woven together with the beautiful threads of the teachings from Scripture were ubiquitous messages of greatness. "Christianity is the greatest religion in the world! And as a pastor, you are called to be great! Lead people, influence them, show them the way to enlarge their territory! You are called to grow your church exponentially! Your church can have excellent programs, a building as large as a mall, a great sound system, and new carpet! You can be a leader—humble, of course—but one that people will follow, making nothing less than your eternal impact on their destiny!"

When I became a Christian, everything changed.

And nothing changed.

THE SIZE OF GOD

Christians believe that at one time, the Divine dwelled in an ovum traveling through the womb of a nervous teenager. But two thousand years later, "small" has become a bad word. Islam is fighting a similar battle with the notion of greatness. Its humble beginnings in Mecca and Medina gave way to expansionist dreams. If God is great, then *we* must be great!

Why do we obsess about a "great" God and a "great" religion? How did the Beloved morph into an emperor?

> *Then, sometime in late childhood or early adolescence, it happens. We realize that the magic and mystery of our existence is finite.*

When we retrace the path of a human being from the womb to the grave, a fear of smallness is inevitable. After birth, all our energies are directed toward survival. We learn to breathe, deal with temperature changes and bowel movements, cope with hunger and thirst, walk, follow directions, and ask for help when we're in trouble. If all goes well, the mystery and glory of human life slowly overtakes us. The universe seems motherly, fatherly, friendly. We feel that we must exist for a good reason. We are going somewhere, right?

Then, sometime in late childhood or early adolescence, it happens. We realize that the magic and mystery of our existence is finite. As our minds mature, we are able to imagine a time in the future when no one who knew us will be alive. It dawns on us that the future could be as though we never were. Everything, including this moment, will one day be without any trace, any proof of our existence. Freud called the experience of having these kinds of thoughts "the trauma of self-consciousness." Milan Kundera, a Czech author, called this burden "lightness" in his book *The Unbearable Lightness of Being*.[1]

Call it what we wish. Trauma. Lightness. This splinter of eternity in our hearts makes us want to matter. We try to compensate for our smallness by pursuing something big. Throughout our lives, we worry about the size of everything we are or own. From the size of our penis or breasts to the size of our car or home to the size of our influence or career to the size of our intelligence or wit to the size of our business or congregation. Once we no longer need to worry about food and shelter, we turn to compensating for our ultimate insignificance.

Everything we do, think, or say is in the service of coping with what theologian Paul Tillich called the "shock of nonbeing." We want the magic, mystery, and naïveté of our childhood back. Right now, for example, writing this book is one of the ways I'm dealing with my smallness. And I say this in the hope that you will think more of me for admitting it!

Throughout modern history, some thinkers and philosophers have called us to stop whining about this state of cosmic affairs. They have said things like "Meaning is absent, and we simply need to learn to live with the fact that we are all infinitely unimportant. This is the truth of human destiny, and faith in any god, idea, or thing is simply a way of coping with the trauma of nonbeing. Especially religion. Religion is nothing but a hysterical and desperate attempt to create meaning in life. Accepting this truth about human existence is not for the fainthearted."

But what if smallness is divine?

What if the ultimate glory of existence is in its smallness, and if the most meaningful role one can ever have is to be invisible, hidden beneath the hubris of our search for something grand?

What if smallness is divine?

On many occasions, Jesus struggled to describe the Kingdom of God to people, who like us wondered about the meaning of what seemed a puny human existence. "Again he said, 'What shall we say Kingdom of God is like, or what parable shall we use to describe it? It is like a mustard seed, which is the smallest seed you plant in the ground.'"[2] Like a small seed in the ground, the Kingdom of God is present. But hidden. Real—but invisible.

The eternal kind of life appears small, insubstantial, *almost* absent.

Why do we religious people so frequently correct each other's view of God by saying, "Your God is too small"?[3]

What if our God is too big?

A QUESTION FROM THE CITY STREETS

"I have a problem with the way God runs the universe," Colleen declared. Without expecting an answer, she lowered her head over a cup of steaming hot chocolate to breathe in the soothing aroma. Our occasional talks were as much a parishioner counseling the pastor as the pastor counseling a parishioner. Colleen, a bright and hopeful young writer, fit into the downtown Manhattan of this millennium as well as my conservative father fit into a Balkan town of the last millennium. As we sat in a corner booth in an uptown coffee shop, I felt satisfied with the way I had helped her grow in her faith over the past several years.

I asked her to tell me more, and she repeated, "I have a problem with the way God runs the universe," then added, "God is too much about God and too little about everyone else. I am not so keen on praising God for his greatness anymore." Her relaxed demeanor said, "Pastor, I am not looking for an explanation here. That's just how things are." She grew up in a family where her father and a brother were both pastors, so she had heard all the answers. I wasn't going to attempt to make another apology for God.

Instead, I told her that I too feel frustrated with a Big God. We talked about the way Native Americans were colonized with the specific Christian theology of the time. They resisted the message because of the courtroom-and-conquest setup of the doctrine offered to them by missionaries preaching the Big God above. God was our judge and Jesus our defender. We were the accused, and Jesus was our way out. That was the good news, plain and simple: God was everything and we were nothing. Missionaries wanted to gift the world with this theological construct, but it didn't resonate with Native Americans. It was a theological language chiseled at some other time and in some other place. The cities of Europe were not wigwam villages. To Native Americans, open skies seemed to offer a better kind of faith.

I made a real effort to understand the God described in the Bible. Having been steeped in existentialist writings and Eastern religions, when I met the Bag (as I described in Chapter Two), I decided the time had come to check out one of the defining books of humankind. To avoid the oppression of the officers, possible time in prison, and ridicule from fellow soldiers, I had a small Bible I read in secret, hiding it in the bushes behind the army barracks, wrapped in two or three plastic bags to protect it from the elements.

As with any other reading, I suspended my disbelief for a time, giving God at least as much chance as I would give any other fictional character. But the Bible was not the easy read I was told it would be. It was an intricate and at times convoluted and contradictory matrix of historical narratives, invitations to social justice, war stories and calls to violence, love poetry, and philosophy about God and life. It was exhilarating, for sure—and I ultimately fell in love with it—but when over the years I sought the help of Christian interpreters to help me distill some of its complexities, I recoiled from what I heard. My main contention was this: God had decided not to create beings equal to God, but lesser ones instead. Why? Why servants and not equals?

> *As with any other reading, I suspended my disbelief for a time, giving God at least as much chance as I would give any other fictional character.*

We are told that the universe was conceived in the mind of a God who could have chosen to create it in any other way. The scenario here seems to be a two-part universe in which one side is subservient and the other side reigns. One side is to serve; the other side is to rule. One side exists to give praise; the other side exists to receive praise. Humans are small, weak, and everything bad, and if you don't like it, you won't be allowed to live with God, who is great, powerful, and everything good.

SUPERIORITY COMPLEX

Have Christians—along with Jews and Muslims—fashioned theology that portrays a God who is on an ego trip? Some of us, God's followers, at times seem to be on one.

I was out with my parishioners when I met Jason, an inspiring young artist making a living in the downtown financial district during the day and painting during the rest of his waking hours. We were munching vegetarian delicacies in Greenwich Village when Jason, sensing our curiosity, graciously shared his issue with Christians.

"In the subway, I'm usually tired. I lean my head back when I ride home. But then these people come through telling me about Jesus. And I'm thinking to myself, 'I just don't have the capacity to consider new ideas right now. I'm worn out; I simply can't. I need this downtime.'" He went on, "After September 11, we found this sacred space in Union Square where in our pain, regardless of our personal backgrounds or beliefs, we would gather just to spend some quiet time with each other. To be one in our grief, you know. But a group of Christians invaded this space with two large loudspeakers. They wanted to be bigger than all of us. And so we lost our place for grieving."

There was an audible sigh of pain around the table as Jason continued, "Why don't religious folk present their ideas where everyone else does? They don't come to book clubs, poetry readings, discussion groups, community service events, and social clubs. There are venues that we as a society set up together for people to share ideas. Why are Christians, and other religious people for that matter, absent from the places where they can't be in charge?

"Because of this, whenever I am attracted to the idea of God and to religious teachings," he continued, "whenever I feel the pull of my heart in that direction, I feel like I must be doing something wrong. I'm afraid I'm being attracted to something that might make me a bad person."

Why are Christians, and other religious people for that matter, absent from the places where they can't be in charge?

His comments transported me back to the morning of September 11, 2002, when one of the Christian family radio networks lined me up for a telephone interview. I was mentally prepared to tell of my experience in New York in the twelve months that followed the terrorist attacks and about the opportunity we had to learn to love the city and its people. But while I was waiting to go on the air, I heard the two cohosts boasting about Christianity, literally patronizing the world. Disoriented and a bit dizzied by what I heard, I realized that I was not ready for the interview at all. As they welcomed me on the air, I panicked and just babbled something to satisfy their warm-up questions, buying some time to think about an answer to the question I knew they would soon ask. And it came right on schedule, with that familiar monochromatic baritone Christian radio voice: "Pastor, tell us, don't you find people in New York more ready to receive the gospel after the tragedy? Aren't they more receptive than ever to the message? Can we take the city for Jesus?"

I gulped—and gulped again. And in the split second before I spoke, I felt the imminent moment of embarrassment that these two conquerors of the world were about to experience.

"No," I admitted nervously. Then I talked without stopping, to prevent interruption until I was finished. "New York is a great opportunity for us Christians to learn. Most of the people here feel that to see the world our way would be a step backward, morally. They see Christians as people not dedicated to following Jesus on earth, but obsessed with their religion. They see us as people who are really not interested in the sufferings on earth like Jesus was but driven with the need to increase the number of those worshiping this Grand Jesus in heaven. They wonder why, of all people, we are the first to rush to solve the world's problems with weapons instead of patience and humility. I learned that it is we who need to be converted after September 11 to the ways of Jesus." And then I stopped.

They didn't ask for clarification. They suddenly started talking about something else, as if I hadn't said anything at all. They cut the interview short, and not even halfway through my time, I was off the air. After hanging up the phone, I turned around in my office swivel chair, staring at some imaginary distant point before me, waiting for the painful feelings to go away, hoping the ticking of the clock on the wall could work like acupuncture and make me feel better.

I was disturbed by my own religion. I realized that it is our superiority complex that makes us an inferior force in making the world a better place.

But as I glanced over a number of books recently published by new authors, I felt a glimmer of hope. These books were discussing the long-standing infatuation of Christianity with power, obtained by hitching its wagon to anything that could help it gain more control at any given time in history—from Emperor Constantine to Emperor Consumerism. I felt comforted by the fact that a new generation of pastors, activists, artists, and writers is being able to give voice to the teachings of Jesus and discover a multitude of remarkable Christian examples of humility—both individuals and communities, past and present—loving and changing the world.

I also realized that in some of our most ordinary rituals and practices, we can see a different God than the one who "takes New York for Jesus."

THE FULL EXTENT OF GOD'S GLORY?

In my Christian denomination, the Seventh-day Adventist Church, we regularly participate in a reenactment of a quite peculiar event from the life of Jesus. In biblical times, a slave or a servant would wash the feet of all guests when they arrived as a practical courtesy, after they had trod unpaved dusty or muddy roads. One of the gospel writers reported that when all of the disciples arrived at the Last Supper, Jesus decided to show them God's glory. He got up from the table, took off his robe, wrapped a towel around his waist, and poured water into a basin. Then he washed everyone's feet.[4]

And that was supposed to show God's glory? "The full extent of it," as the gospel writer puts it.

The Christian mystic Teresa of Avila wrote about the human condition:

> Oh God, I don't love you,
> I don't even want to love you,
> but I want to want to love you!

That's why a basin and a towel are, for me, the most potent symbols of Christian faith. They make me love God.

From this story, I learn that instead of a Cosmic Big Kahuna, God turns out to be a Cosmic Servant, kneeling before creation with hands extended in humble service.

When I first started going to church in Bitola, a small city in Macedonia where I served in the military, I loved to listen to the Preacher. (You'll read more about the little church and the Preacher in Chapter Eight.) Most of the time, I was spellbound by his take on the Bible's poetry and stories. Sometimes, though, I would daydream through the entire service. Once, while I was daydreaming about the soft body of my girlfriend back home, the sermon finished abruptly, and the ensuing commotion woke me up. Everybody was going to another room, where there were buckets of warm water, towels, and white basins.

> *A basin and a towel are, for me, the most potent symbols of Christian faith. They make me love God.*

I fretted. "What is going on? Surgery? Ack, they're going to circumcise someone!" Then it occurred to me that I was one of the youngest males there. I was going to tell them that although I was interested in their religion, I was not ready for that kind of commitment and, besides, I had already been circumcised as a Muslim boy.

But I needn't have panicked. The parishioners sat down in two circles of chairs, women in one and men in the other, water basins on the floor, one in front of each chair. A gentleman gave simple directions and prayed. Without a word, the participants went to a designated place to pour water into their basins and came back to someone in the circle, washed the person's feet, and dried them with a towel. Several of them began humming a song, some old sacred tune.

Each time a person kneeled to wash someone's feet, I felt each one of them telling me as gently as they could, "You will never understand God until you can see God kneeling before you washing your feet."

An old man finally turned to me. "My son," he said, making sure I would hear his weak voice, "This is how God gets things done.

This is how God changes the world. This is God's way." Then he washed my feet.

I did have surgery that morning.

A circumcision.

Of my heart.

GETTING THINGS DONE

I remember when ten of us New Yorkers gathered in one of the coffee shops close to Ground Zero several days after September 11. Each of us expressed our opinion on what needed to be done to stop destructive people from attacking us. At that time, perhaps more than at any other, it was clear to all of us what really needed to be done. Although smoke surrounded us, our minds were clear. We were drunk with pain, grief, anger, and fear. But at that moment, we were sane. We all voted for the subversion of terrorists. And the way to do it was to respect the people, land, culture, and religion from which they are recruiting. Discover and enjoy the goodness and beauty they have. And be thankful for their presence in this world.

Today, any real changes in the world happen this way, through the unstoppable power of humility. Humility is not just about being nice or being virtuous but about knowing how God actually changes the world.

God is subversively small. And God's followers are called to subvert evil with good. If we try to overcome the human obsession with greatness, particularly of a religious kind, by using sheer power, we will become the enemy. Our hate does not confuse and disarm the enemy; our love does. In a spiritual reality (that is, the world as it really is), reliance on power is too weak an approach. It simply doesn't get things done.

The problem is that we have come to believe that humility doesn't work. Showing weakness is considered naïve. For so many of us religious folks, "small" has become disassociated from faith.

But the greatest trauma of being human turns out to be the greatest joy of being human: we are small because we are a part of something larger than ourselves.

We Christians see Jesus on his knees before us, and we don't feel comfortable with it. We don't think it's appropriate. If our divine teacher is small, then our dreams of bigness must be misguided.

> *The greatest trauma of being human turns out to be the greatest joy of being human: we are small because we are a part of something larger than ourselves.*

Paradoxically, those who don't believe in God have a window through which to understand this spiritual reality. Often more than traditional believers, they are aware of how small we humans really are. We religious people have blown our God into a gigantic distortion and ourselves into proportions so grandiose that neither our idea of God nor we fit life as it is. And while we beat our religious chests, secular people live for the present moment, for the joy and pain of ordinary days. And the paradox of their lives is that in coming to terms with the smallness of human existence, they often, without even noticing it, embrace humility. They do good for goodness' sake. And thus they live out the subversive faith we religious people are talking about. While we praise God for God's greatness and ourselves for ours, nonbelievers get things done that—again paradoxically—matter to God more than any talk about the greatness of God.[5]

GENTLE WHISPER

Made despondent by his experience with the faithless people he was among, the great prophet Elijah found himself needing to see God's glory. So God showed up.

The Lord said, "Go out and stand on the mountain in the presence of the Lord, for the Lord is about to pass by. Then a great and powerful wind tore the mountains apart and shattered the rocks before the Lord, but the Lord was not in the wind. After the wind there was an earthquake, but the Lord was not in the earthquake. After the earthquake came a fire, but the Lord was not in the fire. And after the fire came a gentle whisper. When Elijah heard it, he pulled his cloak over his face."[6]

The powerful wind, the shattering of rocks, the earthquake, the fire—none of it made Elijah cover his face. Such a response arose from hearing the gentle whisper that signaled the presence of God.

In contrast, religious obsession with Big God produces Big Religion. Along with many of my religious friends, teachers, and parishioners, I have been growing tired of both.

My God became too big. Burdensomely big.

To many people on the street, Christianity looks like a peculiar subculture, not because it professes to follow a first-century Palestinian carpenter but because while professing to follow a first-century Palestinian carpenter, it acts as though the future of the world depends on the success of the expansionist ambitions of Christians. Maybe we can dismiss this assessment by insisting that the people outside our religion are just finding excuses to avoid submitting themselves to Big God. But what if the real reason we are dismissing their assessment is so that we don't have to submit ourselves to Small God?

Every culture is a mixture of beauty and ugliness, integrity and dishonesty, justice and oppression, kindness and cruelty. The Bible refers to sacred Scripture as a "two-edged sword," something that cuts both ways.[7] And like all cultures, the Christian culture needs a sword to deal with it. It needs surgery every now and then. Until we Christians apply the sword of the Word not only to the culture of the world—cutting it down to size—but also to our own culture, we'll continue to live in an isolated parallel world—a place where the authentic Christian story about a kneeling God is eclipsed by our fantasies of a religion that must rule the world some day soon. Instead of cheering the expansion of our religion as an unquestionably noble goal, we can perhaps quiet down to hear the healing whisper of our God.

Late one night, in one of many conversations with my agnostic friend Mark while walking the streets on the Upper East Side, I wondered aloud about what had happened to us, thoroughly disappointed with myself and my religion. Twenty years after my experience in Macedonia, I find my own life being wrapped up in being nothing more than a well-adjusted citizen and consumer of the empire. Since the beginning of my Christian journey, my life had been moving onward and forward to bigger and better things.

To many people, Christianity looks like a peculiar subculture, not because it professes to follow a first-century Palestinian carpenter but because while professing to follow a first-century Palestinian carpenter, it acts as though the future of the world depends on the success of the expansionist ambitions of Christians.

After venting like this for some time, I fell silent and exhaled. My thoughtful friend waited until he was sure I was done and then said, "It seems to me that Jesus was somewhat different from the kind of religion you describe. The night is young. Let's walk some more. I'm interested in what it might really mean to follow Jesus."

I confessed, "I'm not sure if I can give you a good answer at this moment."

"I didn't ask you a question," he replied.

It was a call to conversation.

Relieved of the pressure to be wise and strong, in charge of the matters of God, walking quietly with Mark, I scanned the gray city streets and saw God right there, a Gentle Whisper, moving graciously among the people, washing their feet, cherishing the world.

DOING WHAT WE KNOW
WILL NOT WORK

An experienced screenwriter, my friend Robin Simmons told me that the best stories, when you boil them down to a line, are about a person or group of people who journey to find what they *want*, and when they find what they want, they realize that that's not what they need. Which, we agreed, can perfectly describe the journeys of Judaism, Christianity, and Islam. We have been journeying in search of the Holy Grail of religious supremacy. We have wanted to be on top. We have assumed that this would somehow make us fulfilled or that people will be won over. But this quest for greatness has left us with unfulfilled believers and an unimpressed world.

We want supremacy, but that is not what we really need. What we really need is to learn to be a part of the whole.

I heard Dallas Willard once say, "You will know you are living the Kingdom kind of life on this earth when you do things you know will not work, and then they do."

What if we were to do what the two of them are suggesting: "turn away from what we want" and "do what we know will not work"?

What if all our fear of nothingness is unfounded? What if Kingdom life dwells in small things? Though we are biased against the small, our prophets were drawn to it. What if giving up on the supremacy of our religion, instead of somehow diminishing it, might allow people to rediscover its beauties?

> *We want supremacy, but that is not what we really need. What we really need is to learn to be a part of the whole.*

Our own Scriptures call us to wait for God, seek God, discern God. I once heard the author Richard Foster saying that this quietness of God is there to tell us something. Maybe it is because God listens more than God speaks. Maybe because the smallness of God is a part of who God really is.

I have come to think of God's perceived absence as a sign of God's faith in us. Yes, *God* believes in *us*. We too should have faith in humanity, trusting that somehow people and God will find one another without our having to picket the world on behalf of the Kingdom of God.

Jesus knew this secret of life when he said that to live, a seed must first fall into the ground and die.[8] Like everything else, in order to live, religion must die. That's the way life works. In order to offer a *living* faith to the world, my religion should die, over and over and over again. From generation to generation. As the old man in Macedonia said to me while washing my feet, "My son, this is how God gets things done. This is how God changes the world. This is God's way."

7

THE BLESSING OF ATHEISM

MY WIFE AND I MARRIED ON JUNE 30, 1990. We also married the next day, on July 1, 1990. My largely secular atheistic family could not fathom the idea of going to a church wedding, talking to my church friends, hearing church talk. They considered themselves so open-minded that they could not conceive of associating with the pious crowd of my wife's family and my new friends. My wife's family, on the other side, did not complain. Actually, they were relieved. It meant they did not have to worry about what they considered twin evils of the world: alcohol and dancing.

Both weddings were stand-alone events involving massive costs. There were two different maids of honor, two different best men, and two sets of vows. Each event denied the existence of the other. In the morning of each of the two days, I went with a different wedding party and met the bride according to prescribed ceremony, then took her to the rituals—the first day in the city hall, the second day in the church. Each party had more than a hundred people in attendance and featured a band and several roasted lambs.

The first wedding, without any reference to God, finished after midnight. My parents assumed that I left with my bride for the night to consummate the marriage. Oh, how I wished! After a year enjoying her voice, a year looking at her face, a year smelling her hair, and a year of occasional excruciatingly limited forays into the forbidden, preceded by five years of self-imposed celibacy during my college days, I was filled with profound love for my wife, my hormones were brimming over, and my mind had become a furnace of desire ready to explode. I had a clear sense of being on a holy mission for the God who said, "And they shall become one body!" But unbeknownst to my parents, the night of the first wedding, we went our separate ways. I slept at a friend's house, and she spent the night at her parent's house.

The New Testament speaks frequently about Christ's Second Coming, and I was, after all, a Seventh-day *Adventist* with that hope burning in my heart; we don't even believe in Hell, a place that would substitute one suffering (eternal) for another (temporal). We were just eager for the world to get better, for the Messiah to return and, in Bob Dylan's words in "Señor," "disconnect the cables" and "overturn these tables" of evil, forever. I thought, "What if Jesus comes tonight? That would be a bummer. I don't want Jesus to come *right now!*" The biblical meaning of the concept of heaven had been thoroughly debated theologically, and I had come to believe that the preponderance of evidence suggested that there would be no sex there. I always thought there would be something much better than sex in eternity, but whatever it was, on that night I did not want it. I lost my religion. I found myself praying for God to delay breaking in and bringing an end to all the suffering in the world for at least one more day so that I could do what I had been dreaming about for years.

And what was the reason I found myself in this ridiculous situation that night, living between two weddings, between two parallel worlds? Instead of embracing the holy awkwardness of two worlds intersecting on an event celebrating life, our families decided it would be better, as they put it, "not to get into a situation." But what that actually meant was never explicitly discussed. Were the evangelical sorts of Christians on my wife's side going to give out booklets describing four steps to accepting Jesus? Were the atheists on my family's side going to have too much to drink and go wild? What would they actually do together? Sing, as people often do at Croatian weddings? What songs? "I Drink to Forget Her" or "We Are Marching to Zion"? The two parallel weddings held a set of assumptions about each other that were as strong as they were unexamined.

Both assumed that atheists and believers must be enemies. It was obvious to both sides that one of them must be terribly wrong. The events surrounding our two weddings was a public enactment of the prejudices lurking in everyone's hearts. But nobody was embarrassed about the sheer silliness of having two segregated weddings. Somehow, the separation of human life into two camps made sense to people.

This was not simply a fear born of social awkwardness. Things went much deeper. History, philosophy, science, and architecture had been erecting the walls of separation for centuries.

FOR, NOT AGAINST

In the atheist society of the former Yugoslavia, as in the rest of Europe, religion was no longer considered, as Marx suggested, "the opium of the people." Apart from its disturbing political manifestations, religion was more like an abandoned opium pipe, on display for tourists who came to see the great, but empty, cathedrals. Europeans were not so much against religion as they were done with religion. They might seek an experience of the transcendent or the sacred, but not in religion. As religions spun out one God management system after another, God himself became at first dangerous, then implausible, and then irrelevant.

"What if this whole 'God thing' of yours is nothing more than a hunch? So what if there is nothing *out there* except deep space and nothing *in here* except our pumping hearts? So what if all we have is our own body, each other, this planet we share, the sky above, and the stories we tell? Would that be so bad? Can you see that as beautiful and full of possibilities?" This, in sum, is what my atheist friends and relatives tell me. They imagine the world not just without religion but without God. To my religious friends, this feels like a plunge into the abyss of meaninglessness. But to my atheist friends, in a secular democracy where religion and God are prevented from hijacking the public square by their interpretation of reality, this is a massive achievement, wonderfully promising.

My friend Rabbi Or Rose, who teaches at the Rabbinical School of Hebrew College in Newton, Massachusetts, taught me about disagreement or *makhloket*, the dialogical model of the early rabbis and Hasidic masters. In Jewish thought and belief, God first provided empty space for life to be created and continues to provide empty space in which creation can continue. According to the rabbis of old, one of the ways the creation continues is through spirited conversations in which we are in a disagreement—the highest form of discourse. When we take a stand and pull the argument in our own direction, we create an empty space between us, a possibility for the emergence of a truly new idea, an unexpected solution, a way forward.

> *According to the rabbis of old, one of the ways the creation continues is through spirited conversations in which we are in a disagreement.*

When we disagree, we pit ourselves *against* one another. But seeing that all of us humans are in this together, we can learn to disagree *for* one another. When we disagree against one another, destruction or even death results; when we disagree for one another, life happens.

All humanity should be included in a conversation that creates.

Including atheists.

Judaism helps us see that for life to work and for good to happen, solutions have to contain their own contradictions, the seeds of their own undoing, the doors to something better that always await us in the future. The rabbis tell us that even the words of the Torah, which they consider a perfect gift from God, are each like a flickering flame, never the same from moment to moment. Or each word is like a rock that can be shattered into pieces to yield new meanings.

For these reasons, opposition is a blessing.

Whenever humans take and hold strong positions with humility, we all gain. That's why rabbinical rulings are published with dissenting opinions (in fact, dissent is often cited first), for regardless of what we consider to be right, we must also honor and preserve the dissenting opinions of others.

> *Whenever humans take and hold strong positions with humility, we all gain.*

Thus for me, atheism is not an enemy of religion but another "rabbi of life." Atheists are our brothers and sisters, our partners and teachers, necessary and good, in a circle with Jews, Christians, Muslims, and people of other religions. They are not to be thought of as guests; they are part of the human household to which we all belong and without whom we would be worse off. What would the world be without those who doubt God? We would be religious people talking to each other in an echo chamber, and the God we believe in would become "God in a box."

Without those who question us, there would be no empty space between us where the truth can be touched—albeit fleetingly—by any one of us.

DISSING AND DISMISSING ATHEISM

We religious people tend to avoid, ridicule, or threaten atheists in a number of ways. We say, most readily, that atheism is just another religion. Since one must believe something in order to doubt something else, all atheists are believers. "Therefore," my Christian peers argue, "atheism has its own objects and ways of worship, its own dogma to teach, and its own priests trying to evangelize others into their either-or choices and—like any other religious fundamentalists—with the same tone of certainty and contempt for others." Atheism, as they see it, insists on forcing a choice between rational and emotional knowing, between the science of life and the mystery of life, calling humanity to an apocalyptic showdown between faith and reason. It wants to clean up the world of those who disagree and create a public square devoid of any options but its own.

Then we say that atheism, by insisting on a purely material view of the world, shuts out the spiritual, mystical, metaphorical, and transcendent, clinging only to what can be controlled, conquered, or manipulated. In other words, atheism is mystically tone-deaf. When I was eight, my sister, Bisera, was thirteen and I loved to hang out in her room with her and her girlfriends. To give me a clue that it was time for me to leave and let them be, she would say, "Hey, little brother, could you please do me a favor and go to the living room and check if I'm there?" I'd gladly jump to comply with her request—until the second part of her statement sank in! The same is true of atheism, religious people think. Behavioral science prods us to dive into life and find meaning, while atheists call on science to insist simultaneously that there is really nothing there. "If the universe will eventually end with a whimper, why bother with such things as justice, beauty, or virtue? With atheism, the magic is gone," religious people say.

In the experience of people who are religious, atheists' claim that they are victims is unfounded. The moneymaking machine of those who write polarizing books about the threat of religion—religion that most religious people neither subscribe to nor practice—would like us to believe that we live under the iron hand of the oppressive dictatorship of priests, pastors, imams, and rabbis. But that is hardly the case. Whereas Voltaire and his cohort opposed the dominant Christian worldview of their day at great expense to themselves, today's atheists operate in a secular culture that dominates the world and buys their books![1] Or so religious people conclude.

> "With atheism, the magic is gone," religious people say.

Then we religious people claim that atheism describes nothing. Since it defines itself in opposition to what it maintains does not exist, it has no substance. At an atheist gathering the other day, a woman told me, "There is so much church politics in our atheist group." She made quotation marks with her fingers while saying the words "church politics."

When I asked her to tell me more about the problem, she continued, "Our leaders have ostracized some members that objected to the whole notion of an atheistic identity. And I have the same problem. Being an atheist is akin to being an anti-unicorn person!" So religious people are asking, "What are you *for*? What *good* are you up to? How do you live *constructively* with billions of religious people on earth?"

> *Dissing and dismissing one another does not create empty space between us. Listening does.*

A religious person might agree with arguments like these and say, "Yeah, this is dead on!" But what's the use of being "dead on" in the world where life wins?

Dissing and dismissing one another does not create empty space between us. Listening does. Perhaps those of us who are religious people can entertain the idea that atheism and atheists are a blessing to us.

WHAT WOULD GOD WANT?

"Blessing" is a religious word meaning "imparting well-being." How can atheism be a blessing to religious people? Is there something of God even in atheism? The answer, I have come to believe, is yes, definitely.

The New Testament book of Acts describes the context of the early church and the beginnings of Christian expansion. Jesus, before his ascension to heaven, informed his perplexed followers, "You will receive power when the Holy Spirit comes on you;

and you will be my witnesses in Jerusalem, and in all Judea and Samaria, and to the ends of the earth."[2] According to the pages that follow this statement, an immense outpouring of love and care for the poor, oppressed, and neglected flowed out of this community into the world, its members being willing to defy an oppressive empire and die for the ideals of human dignity.

Fast-forward a few centuries, and put yourself in the shoes of people encountering what this Christian "witness" had become. Christians arrive on horseback, first pillaging, raping, and murdering, then, over time, overtaxing, Crusading, conducting inquisitions, persecuting, and burning heretics at the stake.

Now imagine this happening in your town, with your friends and family. There are several hundred of you—the few men, women, and children who find a way to escape into the hills. But now you are surrounded. They are behind you, and a river or lake is in front of you. As they arrive, the Christians shout, "We are bringing you the truth. Believe in God!" You think, "We don't have a choice." But you do, and they clearly lay it out for you: "You can either walk into this water, confessing your sins and faith in God, and be baptized, or"—and here is your free choice—"we will kill you." And they reassure you, "Don't say you do not have a choice. You really do."

Surely, most people would choose to live. But if you could escape the situation, what would the Holy Spirit in the book of Acts want you to do? Who is this God you are being asked to confess to and believe in? What kind of choice is this that these followers of God are offering you? Is this God you're being offered, even if he does exist, worth saying yes to? Or should you say no, expecting more from God, if there is such a thing at all?

Now multiply this scene by thousands, by millions. And you could cast Muslims or Jews in the role of oppressors as well. We have all done it: colonized the name of God, set up God management systems, and strip-mined the world for our advantage.

The question then becomes, does God want some people to be atheists?

Can a rejection of God be something that honors God?

Can accepting God in substance (for who God really is) involve rejecting God in concept (for what we believe God is)?

Which choice would be more in line with the essence of Judaism, Christianity, and Islam? What would be more orthodox? What would be more true? Atheism is on to something. Throughout history, God's calls to different groups and peoples have often been perceived by their contemporaries as calls *away* from God.

> *The question then becomes, does God want some people to be atheists? Can a rejection of God be something that honors God?*

Karen Armstrong points out that "atheism has often been a transitional state: thus Jews, Christians, and Muslims were all called 'atheists' by their pagan contemporaries because they had adopted a revolutionary notion of divinity and transcendence." Armstrong then asks, "Is modern atheism a similar denial of a 'God' which is no longer adequate to the problem of our time?"[3]

Rejection of God can be an act of faith.

We are at a point in history when a new view of God is needed again, and many of the emerging believers might be rejected by their fellow believers as atheists. Yet this state of affairs, this betrayal of religion, can be a source of hope. Perhaps we will, as Meister Eckhart suggested, forsake God for the sake of God. And perhaps many of us will be able to exit our religious boxes and meet atheists who have exited theirs. And find ourselves in a new open space.

IMAGINATION AND NOTHING

Ibn 'Arabî wrote, "The sound *Hadith* [Sayings of the Prophet] says: 'Worship God as if you see Him'—such are beliefs. The locus of belief is imagination.... The creatures are bound to worship only what they believe about the Real."[4] My Muslim friend Ali, who lives and talks about God in the most diverse locality in the world, exclaimed passionately in his thick Egyptian accent between singing Christmas songs in his car, "God is an idea." At first, that did not sound right. But the more I listened to him explain it, the more I understood what he meant. He did not mean that God is *just* an idea but that since we cannot really know the Real as we know one another and the material world, our beliefs have to arise through our imagination. All of our knowledge about God is inevitably contingent on our imagination, just as all the ethics of the religious texts are contingent on the ethics of the interpreter of the text. And certainly, in a world where God management systems often manage our imagination, imagining a different kind of God is an act of resistance and hope.

Unquestioning faith is blind faith, and blind faith is no faith at all.

Thank God for atheists.

May they never give up making the world a better place.

Sure, some atheists would like to keep atheism isolated and sealed away from any religious use. They would disagree with any notion of atheism as an enabler of belief! I think that battle is over. As the word "atheism" (literally, "against or without belief in God") implies, religious values and history have blessed atheism by giving it a reason to exist. And now the opposite is true. Atheism can bless religion. *Makhloket* goes on.

The Jewish concept of the divine as *Ayin*, meaning Nothingness—the capital N is deliberate here—is particularly helpful in pointing out the blessing of atheist spiritual sensibilities. *Ayin* is a counterpart of *Yesh*, which is everything that exists, meaning Somethingness. It took Rabbi Lawrence Kushner two hours to get me to an "aha" moment of understanding the concept of *Yesh* and *Ayin*. *Yesh* is not just things in space but also anything that has a border or boundary, a beginning or ending, be it material or immaterial, including holiness and justice—anything that is something. *Ayin* is not emptiness, for emptiness is still a concept, still *Yesh*. *Ayin* is beyond concepts, beyond what we can ever know, a mother lode of existence and beyond existence. In other words, every word that has been written or spoken about God is Something. But God is not Something. God is Nothing—*Ayin*.

> *Then the rabbi added in a more serious tone, "If you are not doubting the existence of God every two weeks, you are theologically comatose!"*

When I asked Rabbi Kushner about atheism, he jokingly said, "Judaism is fine with atheism as long as there is only one God you don't believe in." Then the rabbi added in a more serious tone, "If you are not doubting the existence of God every two weeks, you are theologically comatose!"

Thank you, rabbi.

There is a reason that Jews do not write or pronounce the name of God, and there is a reason Muslims do not use images of God. Refraining from doing so saves them from the human propensity to make God into Something, whether that something is a physical object, an intellectual object, or even the object of our faith. *Because* of our love for God, we question and reject our own understanding of God. Doubt is a virtue of faith. It is a way we hold our sense of God with reverence.

We are called to hold both faith and doubt in the cradle of our devotion. Atheism is therefore a heat-inducing friction that prevents our liquid images of the divine from cooling and solidifying into an idolatrous form.[5] In the nineteenth century, Russian "hole worshipers" understood this propensity of ours and drilled holes in the wall and prayed to them. They prayed to the God Who Was Not There.

My friend Brian McLaren told me of a Pentecostal pastor he met in Uganda. He was one of those fiery charismatic leader types whose "walking in the Spirit" was a 24/7 affair. He told Brian, "All these atheistic books criticizing religion! I bought one. I went home and read it, and God's Spirit came upon me! And it moved me. And the Spirit of God convinced me that the book was true!"

ATHEISM AT ITS BEST

Andrew Sullivan, a journalist (and a believer), contends:

> As humans, we can merely sense the existence of the higher truth, a greater coherence than ourselves, but we cannot see it face to face. That is either funny or sad, and humans stagger from one option to the other. Neither beasts nor angels, we live in twilight, and we are unsure whether it is a prelude to morning or a prelude to night.... [C]omplete religious certainty is, in fact, the real blasphemy.... Doubt, in other words, can feed faith, rather than destroy it. And it forces us, even while believing, to recognize our fundamental duty with respect to God's truth: humility. We do not know. Which is why we believe.[6]

And, I would add, which is why we need those who don't.

Merold Westphal, in his book *Suspicion and Faith: The Religious Uses of Modern Atheism*,[7] makes a thorough argument that atheistic philosophers like Nietzsche, Marx, and Freud have much to say to Christians, and by extension to Jews and Muslims, that they simply cannot say to themselves. We have to admit that much of our religion is made up to serve our own selves, giving us everything from the land of our neighbors to a ready-made sense of purpose.

These towering atheist figures, like the prophets of the Hebrew Bible, call us out of our self-serving use of religion and toward better faith and a better world, which—paradoxically—is what believers say God wants. Arguably, these atheist prophets have done more for our religion than some of our most admired religious leaders.

Maybe the time has come for each one of our monotheisms to adopt another revolutionary notion of divinity, imitating the spirit of Moses, Jesus, and Muhammad—divinity that refuses to be managed, sacredness that spills out of our vessels, God who cannot be contained. Many atheists cannot imagine us laying down our arms, grieving, repenting, and then relearning to live as the created beings we maintain we are. They do not believe such a revolution of generosity among us is possible.

> *Arguably, these atheist prophets have done more for our religion than some of our most admired religious leaders.*

Regrettably, many of my religious friends see atheism at its worst. They see only fundamentalist atheists who use corporate boardrooms, art, government, and academia to impose their own views of reality on others, functioning very much like a fundamentalist religion that worships certainty and has unconditionally surrendered to its dogma. Instead of promoting a secularization that fosters religious pluralism, fundamentalist atheists promote a closed worldview, rid of anything and everything humans cannot understand, control or subjugate, devoid of any options but its own, a place where questions are forbidden, a room without the windows and doors of self-doubt. In the words of the conservative journalist Ross Douthat, "It is one thing to disbelieve in God; it is quite another to never feel a twinge of doubt about one's own disbelief. And just as the Christian who has never entertained doubts about his faith probably hasn't thought hard enough about the matter, the atheist who perceives the Christian God and the flying spaghetti monster as equally ridiculous hypotheses really needs to get out more often."[8]

Or they see only *apathetic* atheists, resigned to giving up on it all and walking away from the mess of the world into a devotion to the newest product, service, experience, or idea offered by the market. Such atheism becomes an empty shell, very much like religion that becomes an empty shell. They offer the world nothing—with the small n.

But there is such a thing as atheism at its best![9]

Atheism at its best participates. It does not simply dismiss religion but engages with it constructively so that the world is better for it. It is an expression of faith in humanity, even faith in religious humanity—however misguided they might be, religious people are human too!—asking the difficult but legitimate questions that religious people dismiss, about scientific evidence ignored by religion, about historical facts forgotten by religion, and about suffering produced by religion. Atheism at its best questions religion while acknowledging the good it brings.

Atheism at its best serves the world as a rebellion against the God offered in the market of religions, a demand that God ought to be more than what or who our God management systems say God is, if God is in fact there at all.

Atheism at its best grabs us by the collar and throws us to the ground, demanding to see lives well lived, forcing us to dig deeper and live up to the best of our own religions.

Atheism at its best hangs on to the hope that our religions have not grasped reality adequately, given what our grasp of reality has brought to the world. It believes that there must be more to the mystery of life than what we have offered.

> *God does not have an ego that can be wounded by our disbelief about God's existence.*

Atheism at its best is a guardian of secularization, a process of creating a common and safe space where world views—including religious ones—can share their treasures and expose themselves to correction by others. It demands that every religion should have the whole of humanity, not just religious insiders, as its ethical community.

Atheists are God's whistle-blowers.

Judaism, Christianity, and Islam need atheists, both those who are constructive and those who are less so. Religion deserves to be challenged. This deserving is of two types. First, religion *deserves the pain* of criticism and correction because of its failures to live up to its own ideals. Second, religion *deserves the blessing* of criticism and correction because it has often been a precious catalyst for justice, peace, and beauty in the world.[10] Recent challenges by atheists should therefore be welcomed by religious people as a chance to see, to grieve, to repent, and then, with renewed wisdom, to act for the common good.

God does not have an ego that can be wounded by our disbelief about God's existence. God, I suggest, would prefer a world where humans love and care for each other and this planet even at the expense of acknowledging God, rather than believing in and worshiping God at the expense of caring for one another and the world.

Atheism at its best locates the mystery of life in this world, this humanity, as the only one we have. It insists that all religion must land where humans live. For them, religion must learn to live on earth. If religion does not work on earth, it does not work at all.

THE VIRTUE OF ATHEISM

To all atheists, I say, "I am sorry."

I will never forget the reaction of a self-proclaimed atheist woman who joined me at one of the large churches in Manhattan to hear a popular pastor tell the audience something to this effect: "Without God, without religion, we are mere egotistic animals fighting for our share, like wolves in a pack. Without faith in the transcendent, we have no basis for morality. Without God, all purpose is lost, and the difference between good and evil becomes meaningless."

To her, that meant, "You as an atheist live a meaningless life. You cannot really be moral. You and your kind are a danger to our society. The world would be better off without you."

In the name of all the clergy, theologians, and believers who have ever said such a thing, I profusely apologize to my atheist friends, family, and readers. Please forgive. Quite the contrary, you bless our world.

Does religion own virtue?

Are religious people *more* likely to be the protectors of the earth's resources, *more* likely to believe in nonviolent solutions to world problems, and *more* likely to care for the poor and the oppressed?

The obvious answer to these questions is no. To which many religious people respond, "Yes, but this is just because the sense of right and wrong of atheists is feeding off of centuries of the development of morality and ethics nurtured by religion. Once that storehouse of tradition is used up, secular societies are going to fall victim to their inherent vacuum of values. If we don't do something, it will all blow up in our faces."

Maybe.

Or maybe the world would be better off with less religion. Or maybe religion needs to transform itself in order to contribute anew to the storehouses of virtue. Or maybe humanism has its own way to supply virtue to our life together. We don't know. But we do know this: atheists have been blessing the earth and its people. This is an empirical truth. And we religious people should look more deeply into our own ethical responsibility to acknowledge what is true.

Moreover, the atheistic theoretical case for a virtuous life is not shabby at all.

While religious people relate their lives to something transcendent, which often means "elsewhere" and "later," atheists are in a position to assume full responsibility for "here" and "now." They cannot avoid, cover up, or postpone solving personal and communal issues in Some Other Time and Some Other Place with Someone Else. All that happens, happens in the present. Every person and moment is precious, unrepeatable, unpostponable—and thus sacred.

In *The Brothers Karamazov*, Dostoyevsky warns against godless moral nihilism with these words: "If God doesn't exist, then everything is permitted." The French philosopher André Glucksmann, in his book about 9/11 titled *Dostoyevsky in Manhattan*, disagrees: if there is a God, he argues, then everything, even blowing up hundreds of innocent bystanders, is permitted. The argument is that once people believe in God, they are in danger of normalizing the violation of any "merely human" constraints and considerations.[11] Atheism thus has a basis to reject anything that instrumentalizes human beings for any purpose, no matter how sacred, as well as to reject anything that neglects the well-being of this present world for the sake of the world to come.

Saint Augustine's injunction to "love God and do as you please" has meant that those who really love God will do the right thing and follow the highest possible ethical standards. I have preached about this notion of Saint Augustine many times, my heart swelling with devotion and the joy of knowing

Our love of God can be a huge liability for those who live around us.

God. But there is a dark side to our devotion. Augustine's words can be like the joke that says, "My fiancée is never late for an appointment, because if she is late, she is no longer my fiancée." Or like wife batterers who believe that they really love their wives. Or like Richard Nixon, who said that "a president can't do anything illegal, because if the president does it, it is not illegal." Our love of God can be a huge liability for those who live around us.

Can this disagreement about virtue be one of those disagreements *for* one another that can create an emptiness between us, a space full of potential? Isn't this an opening for us to reconsider our view of God, a view that may no longer be adequate for the problems of our time?

One evening after family prayers, my daughter Leta, then ten years old, said, "Dad, can I tell you something?" She would usually ask this question just to postpone going to bed. But this was different. "Dad, eternity doesn't make sense to me."

"Why?" I asked.

"It just doesn't make sense, I think. We were all born and then we live and then we all die. That's what makes sense."

"Why can't we all live forever?" I asked.

"We get life as a gift and then others get to live. Plants give up their lives for us. We should give up our lives for others. I like it that way."

"It's all a mystery," I told her, leaving the room and thinking to myself, "What kind of a lame answer was that?" Her questioning can sometimes take me to the edge of the abyss of heresy, wondering whether God would catch me if I should fall. But the abyss was calling me too. Although my daughter was questioning some of the basic assumptions that hold my own belief system together, her observation about death giving way to life sounded orthodox, prophetic, and virtuous to me, something that Jesus would say. Or do. Die so others can live.

AT CAMERA THREE

I subscribe to several MeetUp groups related to atheism, and I attend once in a while. I recently saw an e-mail that said, "Tuesday's meeting is one more opportunity to talk about atheism! We wondered why more people didn't think this way and why the public looked down on it. As we begin a new year, we want to take the next step. We would like to talk about why Atheism, Skepticism, Secularism, and Humanism are not bigger. What can we do about it?"

Every group that has life in it wants to grow. Before embracing transformation as a goal of my religious life, for two decades I was in the proselytizing business. I was convinced that the more people I could help get over the wall and join me, the better the world would be. So before ending this chapter I would like to speak directly to atheists who have been generous enough to make it to this page. I have some proselytizing-expert advice. To borrow a phrase from *The Daily Show*'s Jon Stewart, "Please meet me at camera three."

> *It is really not so preposterous to think that at the end to the day, you too will arrive at a new place, a place where neither you nor believers around you have ever been before.*

First, your motives and methods matter as much as your message. When you disagree with religion, please do not mirror what is worst in religion. That just adds to the misery in the world. Instead, seek to overcome evil with good.

Second, you have something precious we religious people need: doubt. Doubt blesses us. Both faith and doubt are opposites of certainty and therefore part of the same whole. However, the most effective way to help us religious people doubt our certainties is by modeling such doubt. Can you show us the way to self-doubt by questioning at least some of your own assumptions and convictions?

Third, relax. You will not change us. Life will. Life wins, life always wins, and everything will ultimately have to submit to life, including religious people. At the same time, it is really not so preposterous to think that at the end of the day, you too will arrive at a new place, a place where neither you nor believers around you have ever been before. You too are called to let life win.

Fourth, step out of your groups and meet your religious neighbors. Stop at their door, their office cubicle, their turf. Perhaps invite them for a walk together. Talk about food and wine. If you are daring, come into their kitchens, sit at their tables, let them pray over you, eat with them, and have a good time.

Can there be a greater power trip than believing that everyone is on a power trip except oneself?

Finally, dig deeper in the well of your tradition. One of your distinguished teachers—whom, by the way, many of us believers quote and admire—Friedrich Nietzsche, maintained that every truth is a tool in the hands of those in power. Please don't cling to the irrational belief that you are an exception, somehow spared from this human curse. Can there be a greater power trip than believing that everyone is on a power trip except oneself?

All I want to say to you is that you know, I know, we all know that if we don't turn life on this planet around—all of us *together*—we are heading for a disaster. The power struggles help no one.

ASKING BETTER QUESTIONS TOGETHER

To the very end of his life, Sigmund Freud was an uncompromising atheist, describing in his book *The Future of an Illusion* that belief in God is a "collective neurosis."[12] But in his last and difficult-to-publish book *Moses and Monotheism*, he recognized that the poetry and the promise of religion exist along with its shadows.[13] He argued that pure and undiluted faith in One God (Freud singled out Judaism as its only authentic expression), instead of being the so-called opium of the people, helped free humanity from bondage to the immediate, empirical world, opening up fresh and renewed possibilities for human spirit and practice. He argued that people who can worship what is presented in symbolic terms practice the ultimate exploration of the invisible inner life. For Freud, faith in God opened a gift of inwardness and imagination.[14]

> *For Freud, faith in God opened a gift of inwardness and imagination.*

In a letter to Romain Rolland, his friend immersed in mysticism, Freud wrote, "How remote from me are the worlds in which you move! To me mysticism is just as closed a book as music. I cannot imagine reading all the literature which, according to your letter, you have studied. And yet it is easier for you than for us to read the human soul!"[15]

What matters here is that we acknowledge both the good and the bad, the light and the shadow, in the other and seek a way of being together in this world. Greg Epstein, a friend and a humanist chaplain at Harvard University who wrote a book titled *Good Without God*,[16] said in one of his interviews:

> If people take only one thing from my work, let it be the idea that an authentic, passionate, committed humanist—and yes, atheist—must accept the dignity of other beliefs. Some atheists want to erase religion, the way some religious

fundamentalists want to erase humanism. My humanism is an embracing philosophy. It says, let's understand ourselves enough to know why we disagree, then let's trust ourselves enough to care about each other and work together toward common goals.[17]

The stingy polemics of religionists who defend religion at all costs and antireligionists who fight against it at all costs are not helping the world. Their identities depend on a conflicted world. Instead of leading us to generosity to others and greater hope for the unknown future, instead of enlightening and inspiring us to disagree *for* one another, religionists and antireligionists are moving us into a new dark age, both of them *using* God and bringing an end to the conversation.

For too long, we have been arguing over the question "Does God exist?"

Exist in what? In space? In time?

> *The stingy polemics of religionists who defend religion at all costs and antireligionists who fight against it at all costs are not helping the world.*

We use these notions of physical existence or nonexistence to somehow remove our subjective experiences in order to objectify, externalize, and contain God. Both sides would love that kind of certainty! It makes God Something, captured by our notions of being, belief, and existence. That way, we can choose to count or discount God. Or worse yet, utilize God.

We need to develop better questions.

I propose three of them, as a start, each one with more potential than the one that has fatigued us all, each one helping us begin to create the empty, pregnant space we need. Here's what we can ask each other:

1. What do you believe in when you believe—or not believe—in God?

2. What can you do to seek out, protect, and hear those who subvert your ideas about the God you believe in or don't believe in?

3. How can we turn the tensions between us into something that is life-giving rather than destructive?

Atheism does not have to be the end of the mystical; it can be the beginning.

Religion does not have to be the opium of the people; it can be the poetry of the people.

Both faith and doubt are opposites of certainty and therefore part of the same whole that refuses to see all but the obvious. To end either of them would be to end imagination.

Faith imagines. And so does doubt.

We both have both.

And we are better together.

At the time of my wedding, my family and I did not believe that we can possibly be better together. We organized our two weddings without the conviction and courage to stand up together against forces that thrive on dividing human life.

Yet, there were exceptions at our two wedding parties. My uncle Franc and his wife, Gordana, who came from Germany for the occasion, stepped over the line and attended our religious wedding. The absence of dancing puzzled them to no end, but that did not stop them from telling jokes and hugging everyone. Also, I smuggled several of my Christian friends into our first wedding, telling my dad that these were my "friends from the city," including Tihomir Žestić, a friend who cared for me and taught me about God during the two years of exile from my family when we shared hunger and cold in our student days, eating food he brought to the city from the village where his parents lived.

At this party, he crossed the line and danced with the atheist crowd, risking his entrance to Paradise. Since Seventh-day Adventists are seriously dance-challenged, he found great difficulty translating music into body movements. I watched him randomly jerk his body as if he was stomping bugs on the dance floor. One of my amused friends said, "I think he has a hidden Walkman playing a different song!"

But the beauty of the sight of him energetically celebrating life with unbelievers with such abandonment brought me to tears. My atheist friends loved it. It was the best dancing I have ever seen!

8

ONE WORLD AT A TIME

A BAPTISMAL POOL IN THE BASEMENT of a small church in Macedonia was the place of my beginning. In hiding, away from the prying eyes of the military police, I was immersed in the water of life.

Our barracks were located in the small city of Bitola in today's Republic of Macedonia, nine miles from the border with Greece. That evening, the compound was at peace. It housed four thousand weary soldiers, both new recruits—crying themselves to sleep and hoping for relief from their harsh newfound reality—and soldiers near the end of their term, drinking themselves to sleep on plum brandy smuggled onto the premises. The Bag and I jumped the fence and, under cover of the night and with quick, silent moves born of experience, made our way to a hokey little church downtown.

My journey to the baptismal pool had started six months earlier. Late in the evening, week after week and then day after day, the Bag and I dodged patrols on the border between the military and civilian worlds and climbed the compound fence to visit the Preacher's home. Stevan the Preacher was a big man, a former gang leader, his tattooed arms now covered by a businesslike suit. His kindness was fresh, humorous, and steady. When I saw Stevan and his wife, Anda, rolling down a grassy hill in an embrace—he very big and comfortably round in his suit, she very small, with long hair, in her church dress—then walking up the hill and picking a couple of rare medicinal herbs to take home with them, I liked him immediately.

The rest of the congregation did not impress. The Bag and the Preacher invited me to a worship service. That was a big thing for me. I was entering a whole new world of crazies.

The first person to approach me that day, and whenever I came after that, was an old farmer, thin and short like one of the dried chili peppers he produced, always dapper in a worn-out but grand suit and tie. Every week, he stepped up to me, looked me straight in the eye, and submitted a report on his weekly vision of Jesus. Usually on Tuesdays around noon while working in a hot summer field, he claimed, Jesus appeared and talked to him in person. He updated me on the latest news delivered to him from the heavens. I was advancing fast—barely a month into my journey through the land of crazies, I had only two degrees of separation from Jesus himself!

In the church was a large woman who suffered from hypertension. Everyone would scurry around helping her, bringing a glass of cold water, assisting her up and down stairs, asking if she needed anything. Her tiny husband, a factory worker, did the cooking at home and cleaned their one-bedroom government-assigned apartment while she sat on a couch the whole day moving from snack to snack. Church members referred to her as the Head Deaconess. I had no idea what that meant, but I noticed that whenever she heard her title in conversation, her face would beam with pride and everyone would be happy for her.

Two sisters in their late teens were in the group. The older one had stopped growing at age six; the younger one had big eyes. They were quite a sight, both clinging close to me after coming to the barracks and obtaining permission from the army to take me out for a day, claiming they were my "sisters" (by which they meant "future sisters in Christ"). I never met the parents, but the girls seemed to be a family in their own right.

I also met Macedonian rednecks, a young couple with a string of children behind them. It appeared they had not spent much time in school and had little ability to carry on a conversation with city folks. From what I could tell, they mostly grew peppers and made children.

The Preacher had a son and a daughter. The daughter proved to be a quiet girl with unsettling dreams about God that she could not quite understand. The son had a brittle bone syndrome and suffered greatly.

Finally, I noticed a man who came only occasionally to worship services, since it took him a whole day of brisk walking to cover the distance from his remote village to the church. His body and face were scarred by burns from several occasions when the villagers had smeared him with bacon and poured wine over him, ridiculing his adherence to a version of Jewish food laws and abstinence from any alcohol (Adventists regard body as important as soul—two parts of the same whole), and then had thrown him into a bonfire to see if God would protect him. When he came to church, he would be humming old Christian hymns as he walked confidently down the aisle between the pews. This was the only place he could live freely, where Jesus and his friends were his consolation.

Søren Kierkegaard said that our greatest doubt comes just before we believe.

I decided that these people were not for me, the chili pepper man who talked to Jesus, the red-faced Head Deaconess, the midget, the unschooled couple with a cartload of children, the fanatic from the flames. I was into yoga, pot, and philosophy. I was different from this motley crew of Jesus people. I didn't need a little church on the Balkan prairie to teach me the meaning of life. I read Herman Hesse and Carlos Castañeda.

I was full of myself, and I called it spirituality.

Two months after my first visit to the church, the Bag gave up on me. He took me off his prayer list. Why waste prayer? But it was too late. I had this nagging thought—a creeping conviction actually—that these people were doing something right. And I could not shake off the question: What was it? In every way I had learned to measure life, these people were just not making it. But there was something at work in and among them that mattered more than anything else I had experienced. What was it?

I was full of myself, and I called it spirituality.

This unanswered question gripped my heart and would not let go. It pressed on the splinter of eternity lodged there, and I did something I had not been able to do before. I forgot to think about myself. I failed to judge and constantly divide people and experiences into two bins, one reasonable and acceptable and the other the crazy bin. The question "What is it with these people?" came to me from an inner unexplored space and swept away every other concern I had. The constant chatter of my usual inner monologue quieted down.

And created a clearing.

That's how I came to the water of life that night. Six months after I had stepped into the little church for the first time, we all went downstairs to the small baptismal pool. The dusty, musty church basement, where boxes, bicycles, garden tools, and old church furniture were stored, had been transformed for the occasion.

All the stuff had been pushed aside to create a path to provide access to the water.

Under dim lights, we stepped around the little pool in the ground. The water shimmered with life, and Spirit of God hovered in the void above it.

The Preacher broke the silence by reading from the Gospel of Luke: "When all the people were being baptized, Jesus was baptized too."[1] Ever since hearing this deceptively simple statement, I have wondered about its meaning. Why would Jesus be baptized? To wash away his sins? Jesus was not supposed to have any sins. Could baptism be an invitation into something that reaches beyond managing sins?

Slowly descending into the pool and then standing there with water up to my waist, dressed in a white baptismal robe, feeling safe next to the Preacher, waiting for the feeble but confident voices to finish a long, soft Christian hymn, I did not feel that I was joining a church or becoming a part of the story of God's people over the ages or even beginning a new life. Instead of creating something new, my immersion in water seemed to connect me

Why would Jesus be baptized? To wash away his sins? Jesus was not supposed to have any sins.

with something that was thousands, even millions of years old. I was connecting with the beginning of everything, with primordial life, weaving the story of my life with the great story that began before Christianity, before religion, before the Bible, when we were all one.

WHAT WAS JESUS SELLING?

When Jesus left the home of his parents, he not only entered the public life of first-century Palestine but also entered the marketplace of world ideas, and as in every market, there were buyers searching for a good product.

He did not offer many explanations. Instead, he offered a way of life. And that's what people around Jesus wanted to know. About life.

They came with questions. "Rabbi, why should we follow you? Why should we dedicate our lives to your way? Give us a good reason."

And today, people considering Christianity ask the same question: What will I get out of following Jesus?

"Following Jesus will empower you, surround you with more friends, give you more abilities and more fulfillment, with eternal life as the ultimate reward," I along with other pastors used to say. Nowadays, realizing how misguided these promises of prosperity can be, many Christians dismiss the question altogether. "Don't ask 'What will I get out of following Jesus?'" we correct them. "Instead, you should come to God for God's sake, not for yours. Don't come to God to *use* God."

But that's not an answer.

People, with only one life to live, *should* be asking what they can get out of following anyone. Why not? It's a fair question. This life is a temporary experience, a very precious gift, and we need to choose well how to use it. It's all we have.

So what will I get out of following Jesus?

At first, people didn't know what to make of Jesus' answer. He talked about the Kingdom of God that saturates our physical world, visits every person, sustains every relationship, gives life to every plant, and blesses every person and every thing. Even stones were not left out of his awareness of life. Where others saw divisions all around, Jesus saw oneness. Heaven and earth. Suffering and joy. Us and them. Jesus addressed his followers' fearfully-divided lives and brought them peace. "Everything will be okay in the end," my fridge magnet says; "if it's not okay, it is not the end." Jesus really believed that.

The hope that Jesus brought into their lives was at the very same time a call: "Come and follow me."

"Follow you where?"

His answer was not what they expected. First, he answered with what he was *not* calling them to, what he was *not* promising. To a person who wanted to be his follower, he replied that while foxes have holes and birds have nests, he and his followers might not have a place to lay their heads. He said his message might bring them not peace but strife, even in their own families. To future followers, among other things, he offered the possibility of persecution, even death at the hands of the empire. The early church continued to issue the same disclaimer. Jesus was serious about setting people's expectations right: "If anyone would come after me, he must deny himself and take up his cross and follow me."[2]

Despite all this bad marketing, from the first disciple through all of Christian history to this very day, people have wanted what Jesus offered. Why? Why would anyone want to be deprived of a place to lay their head? Why would anyone want to disturb families or strain friendships? Why would anyone walk a path that could lead them to persecution and death? Why would anyone want to carry a cross?

Because of the treasure.

Jesus told a story about a man who found a treasure buried in the field, sold everything he had, and then bought the field.

Because of the pearl.

Jesus told a story about a man who found a pearl of extraordinary value, so he sold everything he had, bought the pearl, and walked away with the joy of getting a great deal.

Clearly, Jesus offered something for us to buy. Whether by conscious choice or by drifting, we all give our lives to something. We have all received this unearned right to live, and we have to choose what to do with it. I was baptized because I sensed that Jesus offered something of unsurpassed value. I say "sensed" because I couldn't name it for ten years.

Jesus offered a single incentive to follow him; it was woven into all he said and did.* Here is how I would, after twenty-four years of

---

*Some sample texts: John 13:34, 35; John 15:5–17; Matthew 5:43–45; Matthew 22:37–40; Romans 13:8–10; 1 Corinthians 13; Ephesians 3:17–19; and 1 John 4:7–21.

following, summarize his selling point: "Follow me, and you might be happy—or you might not. Follow me, and you might be empowered—or you might not. Follow me, and you might have more friends—or you might not. Follow me, and you might have the answers—or you might not. Follow me, and you might be better off—or you might not. If you follow me, you may be worse off in every way you use to measure life. Follow me nevertheless. Because I have an offer that is worth giving up everything you have: you will learn to love well."

You will learn to love well.

This is a deceptively simple string of words.

It takes time for the beauty of this offer to break into one's being. Once you take a look at this offer from every angle, once you start to compare it with any other offer in life, with any other treasure or pearl, any other destination, you begin to realize that nothing in this world can possibly compare.

That is the answer I have found, the treasure, the pearl I gave my life for. That is what I have experienced in a hokey little church and why I have decided to follow Jesus and, as the Christian hymn says, have not turned back.

LOST IN MAPS

The only way to hold the pearl of one's religion is with life itself.

There was a time when we clergy were obsessed with writing down the vision of our congregation and organizing it to achieve our goals. We would take days to talk, months to strategize, and years to implement the plan. At the time, I learned to imagine my church community as a herd of people circled by a gigantic rubber band. I imagined that without a vision and a mission statement for us to rally around, all our energies simply bounced around the system and canceled each other out. The band might stretch and contract, but we would never actually move together, because everyone moved in a different direction. That's why we clergy wanted our vision statements. We produced a map and put it in everyone's hands.

The assumption guiding this approach is that life is mostly chaos and has to be reined in. People need to be organized out of "life as it is" and into the practices and purposes of our religious organizations. The natural web of our personal and communal lives was not to be trusted, so we created new environments for them. For us all to move in the same direction and not waste our energies, we had to ask people to give up "life as is" and be discipled into prescribed organizational behaviors such as worship services, small-group meetings, outreach ministries, and myriad programs.

The Kingdom of God that Jesus spoke of was out of the reach of our people where they were, but it would be within their grasp where we were taking them.

Many of us, especially in the West, have been collecting maps like these all our lives. To explain our human experience, discover the meaning of it all, and set goals, we have been looking for the right map, comparing our maps, and arguing about which map is correct. This left many of us outside "life as is."

Walking through the landscape of life became a luxury we could not afford.

We got lost in maps.

Paths are made by walking, and when we get lost in maps, we stop walking. In contrast, Jesus—and most other founders of religions around us—taught a way of life, a way of being, a way of journeying through the landscape itself.

The problem with maps is that they focus on a destination, and we start to live for the place and time of our future arrival. Life loses its immediacy.

The journey *is* the destination.

> *Paths are made by walking, and when we get lost in maps, we stop walking.*

Every once in a while, I hear people reacting to what they see as cliché, saying that romanticizing the journey is misguided. "A journey that leads nowhere is not worth taking! We have to have maps so we can get *somewhere*! What is the value of a journey if it takes you where you don't want to be? We are looking to eternity with God. That's our destination!"

But in eternity, there is no such thing as arriving. If we *plan to arrive* somewhere, we are not ready for time without end. This life and the life to come are part of the same whole. Dallas Willard writes:

> I am thoroughly convinced that God will let everyone into heaven who, in his considered opinion, can stand it. But

"standing it" may prove to be a more difficult matter that those who take their view of heaven from popular movies or popular preaching may think. The fires of heaven may be hotter than those in the other place.... There is a widespread notion that just passing through death transforms human character.... Just believe enough to "make it." But I have never been able to find any basis in scriptural tradition or psychological reality to think this might be so.[3]

Willard shows how the life we live and the life to come are both part of the same journey. The landscape is the destination. God is here, in the landscape. The pearl is available here and now in "life as it is." We can learn to love the actual life we have now. How many billions of years do we need to live before we realize we've already arrived where the pearl can be found?

Life—not religion or theology—is the medium of love. The only maps worth having, therefore, are those that send us onto the landscape of life. Moreover, people who know how to love well are our guides and the embodiment of the Christian story, beliefs, and values, regardless of whether they have the Christian map in their hands.

On a TV talk show I saw a long time ago, a prominent Christian and a prominent atheist were in agreement that being a good human being is what we all should be about, before we are ever Christians, atheists, or anything else. The host then took calls, and a rather eager voice on the phone insisted that "Christianity is about grace. Christianity has nothing to say about being good." This declaration that Christianity has nothing to say about being good landed on the audience with a thump. Both the host and the atheist empathized with the Christian in the studio, who was struggling to keep his composure.

Yes, Christianity is about grace, and I believe magnificently so, but "Christianity had nothing to do with being good"?

People are not looking for someone to show them how to escape life; they are looking for practicing sojourners and communities to help them walk the landscape of life.

Perhaps this man's comment expressed something I myself would say to others about Christianity. But when I heard this from another person, and stated in public like this, it felt as though God's hand pressed me. My heart started pounding, and my eyes welled. This caller, a well-meaning Christian, got his hands on the map with the instructions on how to get to heaven, and forgot that Christianity is largely about life itself, this life, on this earth.

Too much of religion has been about cartography.

The world is suffocating in maps.

People are not looking for someone to show them how to escape life; they are looking for practicing sojourners and communities to help them walk the landscape of life.

BETTER NEWS

Inability to articulate religion in terms that captivate the imagination of believers and nonbelievers alike is a widespread problem, particularly in the West. There is something impotent about contemporary Christianity, to take my own religion as an example, and it has to do with its inability to reimagine the answer to the question "What do I get for following Jesus?" For too many Christians, the answer is "heaven." The reward will arrive one day when we leave the landscape of life as we know it. While the promise of heaven certainly offers consolation to the suffering and wronged on this earth, heaven without the ability to love would be nothing but an extension of suffering and injustice into eternity.

Will Christianity continue to define itself by a set of maps of how to leave this place, or will it open up and find its cause along with others who are also willing to seek goodness and grace in the landscape of life? Will religion hunker down, insisting on the answer that locates an eternal kind of life in another kind of world, or will it walk back into this world as a partner and learner participating in the goodness outside its boundaries?

Nothing determines the present boundaries of Christianity like the term "good news," a translation of the New Testament Greek word *evangelion*. Understood in a lopsided way, "good news" came to mean the news that believers could go to some other place someday. We are realizing what has been obvious for a long time to those looking at Christianity from the outside. The apex of our self-centeredness is an obsession with getting to heaven after we die at the expense of excluding God's life from this world. The earth is a waiting room; real life is to be found elsewhere and later.

At times, as now, I feel that my characterizations of Christianity are bordering on caricature. Someone said that we tend to demonize what is familiar and romanticize what is foreign. I am definitely guilty of that.

The truth is that Christianity has been offering a far larger dream to individuals.

To get to heaven is good news, but not good enough.

> *The earth is a waiting room; real life is to be found elsewhere and later.*

For many Christians, Jesus had very little to say about heaven in the four gospels. His good news was better.

The Talmud tells of a rabbi who threw a great party in his home to which he invited all of his friends, family, and followers. A friend came to his house wondering, "Why is there a celebration here? No one has been born or married. Why are you all singing and dancing?"

The rabbi answered, "Yesterday, I was going about my business with the elders of the village when a woman approached and asked me to come to her home because her daughter was ill. I could not interrupt my appointment with the village elders, so I told her to go home and wait. When I got to her home that evening, to my great dismay, the girl had died. I went home, and during the night, I woke up and prayed. I said to God, 'Please let me resurrect the girl tomorrow! If she lives, may my name be taken out of the Book.' And God accepted my offer. This morning, I went to the girl's house and resurrected her. And now I am celebrating with all my students and all of my family and friends."

"What are you celebrating?" his friend asked.

His face beaming, the rabbi answered, "I am celebrating my freedom. For the first time in my life, I can serve God not for the sake of any rewards but for the sake of my love for God."[4]

Many years of my Christian life have been spent dwelling on how I can be admitted to heaven one day. I would be admitted by grace. Good. And people, religions, philosophies, and ideologies that have relied on anything else but the grace of God were attempts at saving themselves by their own works. Okay, I get that. God is God, and nobody can force God to save us. When I first excitedly explained this good news of going to heaven to my mother back in Croatia, her reaction puzzled me. She was not impressed. She made a face as though there were something a bit stinky in the room.

But there is a better kind of Christianity, a more authentic one, one based on the life and teachings of Jesus. Our sins are managed, our eternity is secured, our acceptance is unconditional—but this is not the offer! Once we have been unconditionally accepted, once we own up to our dark side and dispel it with God's light, then the journey is just beginning. We can now love freely for the sake of participating in the joy of our master and not to make ourselves acceptable or valuable. Then we are ready to love for love's sake and become useful to God and the universe.

During my college years, I wanted to be a substitute teacher and needed a background check at the local police station. They asked me questions, checked the databases, took my fingerprints, and cleared me. But every time the school called me to come and teach, I never went. I was too busy. "I have a previous appointment," I would say honestly to the person on the phone asking me to come in. For four years, I never set foot in the classroom. In the same way, over and over again, we can spend our whole religious career visiting the celestial police station and checking our clearance without actually entering the calling.

Heaven is not the calling. Life is the calling. And eternity is just a part of life.

Heaven is not the calling. Life is the calling. And eternity is just a part of life.

In Redlands, California, we had a street fair every Thursday. And every week, there was a particular Christian group there with a stand full of banners accosting people who passed, asking every single person the same question, "If you died tomorrow, would you go to heaven or hell?" Their zeal made a lot of people nervous.

When approaching their zone of operation, I would turn my head the other way and speed up my gait. But one day, one of the men stepped in front of me, blocking my way, his face filled with concern. "If you died tomorrow," he asked, "would you go to heaven or hell?"

Trapped, I blurted out back into his face, "I don't care!"

What this really meant was that I was tired of even thinking about the question. Exhausted actually. Maybe an eternal kind of life is going to include eternity. That did not matter anymore. Loving well in this life, even without eternity, would still remain "the pearl of great value." But eternity without the eternal kind of life would be worthless.

Knowing that I was a pastor, a man at the booth was flustered at my answer and retorted impatiently, "Oh, one day, when the judgment comes, you will care!"

I didn't know what to say to him, so I blurted out what Jesus said to Peter, who tempted him to abandon his mission, "Get behind me, Satan!"[5]

I consciously decided not to care whether I will ever be in a place such as paradise. In fact, if God's cause can be helped by taking away my life in paradise (then) to effect some good on earth (now), God is welcome to do so. And I have unshackled my life by telling God so.

Recently, I asked an old rabbi from Brooklyn here in New York, "Rabbi, what is Judaism teaching about eternal life? I don't hear you talking about it much. I need to know."

He said confidently, "One world at a time, my friend, one world at a time." I realized that Jesus, a Jewish rabbi, would say that.

Now I pray, "Dear God, I want to be a lover of you, myself, people, and all of life. Help me learn to live one world at a time."

WITHIN A CATHEDRAL

However wonderful it might be, eternity is a secondary product. Neither Christianity nor God's acceptance nor eternity is the pearl. The pearl is the Kingdom of God, an invitation to learn to love well. And the school of that love is life—our ordinary life, the one we have, not the one we wish we had.

Only life can change our theology. My favorite seminary professor, Jon Paulien, spoke to a small group of us over a lunch about what he called "double hermeneutics" (hermeneutics is the way we interpret something). When the early church faced a decision about whether or not to accept the conversion of non-Jews to Christianity, a conference of leaders gathered and struggled with a question: Do Gentiles have to become Jews before they can become Christians?

> *Neither Christianity nor God's acceptance nor eternity is the pearl. The pearl is the Kingdom of God, an invitation to learn to love well.*

When they heard that Gentiles were being baptized, the group didn't know what to do. It is difficult to overstate the agony of this group. The Bible they read said one thing ("no, they can't"), and now reality—the very life they experienced—contradicted it ("yes, they can"). They were realizing, perhaps more clearly than ever, that life cannot be dismissed. Not just religious texts but life, too, requires honest interpretation.

A glimpse of the difficulty of that moment can be seen in the agony of some Christians dealing with the Bible and homosexuality today. Some Christians seem to be interpreting the Bible in a way that does not help them love well. Whether we condone homosexuality or not, something is as wrong with our interpretation of this issue as it was wrong with the interpretations that sanctioned religious wars, wiping out Native Americans, supporting slavery, and oppressing women.

What to do with the Gentiles was the first of such dilemmas for the early church, and what happened is enormously instructive.

After hearing the reports at the church council, James, the brother of Jesus, stood up and said, "Brothers, listen to me." After the group quieted down, he said, "God showed his concern by taking from the Gentiles a people for himself. The words of the prophet are in agreement with this, as it is written..."[6] James then quoted the old prophets. Up to that point, the young Christian church was interpreting the reality of its adherents' new lives through the eyes of Scripture. But this was different. The church now had to learn to interpret Scripture through the eyes of reality. Gentiles? Members of God's Kingdom? Yes, reality was confirming that, and Scripture *had* to be reinterpreted.

This was a metamorphosis of theological methodology.

Instead of disregarding the landscape of life, these early Christians had to learn to reread the sacred map of Scripture. If the map, however sacred, and reality are in disagreement, it becomes clear that we can't use the map to violate reality. To do evil for the sake of the text would violate the text. The text is about life. And life wins. Life always wins. Like water, it will always find its way.

We have this life, you and I, with one another. That's the only fact we know. Everything else, we believe.

Today, we are on a similar threshold. We are asked again to answer the question "What do I get for following Jesus?" On this threshold of the Christianity of the twenty-first century, the old answers are gone, and emptiness is hovering over us again. A new reading of Scripture is emerging, and a new theology is being born, one that honors the only thing that is indubitably real and sacred: life. We have this life, you and I, with one another. That's the only fact we know. Everything else, we believe.

To see the beauty of Christianity as a "way of life" instead of a "way out of this life," one needs to take time. My friend Ante Jerončić, a professor of religion at Andrews University, told me that the greater the truth, the more time one's eyes need to adjust to be able to see it. It's like entering a cathedral, he says. At first, it's dark and quiet. That's why one has to wait, simply looking and listening, until one's eyes and ears learn to see and hear. Once our senses adjust to the new environment, we start discerning the beauty, the depth. Darkness gives way to colors and shapes. Silence begins to give way to sounds. And the place becomes beautiful.[7] Again, Jesus would say, "Let those who have ears to hear, hear," calling us to hear deeper truth in the gentle whispers of God without and within us.

What was right about those people in the Balkan prairie church where I was baptized? They were learning from Jesus how to love. Christianity, with all of its texts, traditions, and practices, was nothing but a treasure box holding the story of Jesus. Ever since, this community has stayed a beacon on the open seas, guarding me from getting lost in my religion.

When I was buried in the water of life and rose from it, I became sane for the first time. With new eyes and new ears, I began learning to adjust my senses to the Kingdom of God, the world as it really is. Now I am seeking God, not out of this life, but deeper and farther into it.

As in the beginning, the Spirit of God still hovers over the baptismal waters. Eternal celestial lights and sounds are not held back from us. They ricochet through the cathedrals of our religious traditions. For me, it was Jesus who helped me see and hear them now, in this life, saying, "Follow me, and you might be better off—or you might not. But follow me anyway. I offer you something that is worth everything: you will learn to love well." Jesus loved so well that he died for something greater than himself. So should religion that claims to follow him.

9

WHEN MY GOD BECOMES OUR GOD

IN THE SECULARIZED EUROPE WHERE I GREW UP, the vast majority of people didn't subscribe to any traditional religious beliefs. During my high school years, I concurred. We, the majority, were open-minded, obviously. They, the religious people, were emotionally or intellectually weak at best. At worst, they were a danger to society at large. Either way, they were not to be trusted with responsible jobs or positions of power.

"Who could be safe with a person in authority who trusts some nebulous idea like God, rather than rational thinking, when making decisions?" we asked each other, shaking our heads.

That's one reason why, when I decided to become a Christian, my family threw me out. They wanted me to learn a bitter lesson about religion and be better for it. Although my father had a strong ethnic identity as a Muslim, he wasn't really a believer.

Strange as this may sound, he was both a committed Muslim and a committed enemy of religion. He simply wanted to live a good life—which, as I've said earlier, meant living with Pleasure and Honor—without being harassed by religious people. He saw the world divided into two camps: normal people and religious people. Now I had crossed the line and gone over to the other side. After four months of anxious coexistence, tears, threats, and bribes, he saw expulsion from home and family as the last resort. He laid out my options and declared, "It's either us or them."

"If you go to church next Saturday, don't come back," he said. That Thursday, I packed my belongings into a friend's car and left. I was a prodigal son leaving my earthly father to be with my heavenly father. What a choice.

I left what used to be "us" to join "them."

Although the tears, the raised voices, and the long arguments were behind me, leaving home was far more difficult than I thought it would be. I found myself moving from one apartment to another among church members in Zagreb who were willing to help me, but I missed the warmth, touches, sounds, tastes, and smells of my family.

Yet no matter how difficult I found this two-year experience of homesick wandering, something else happened as a result of my conversion that was far more terrible.

My world shrank.

I let hundreds of non-Christian people drift away from my life. I found myself hanging around Christians almost exclusively. I became a follower of the One God, but my world remained divided. For non-Christians, we Christians were "them." For us Christians, the atheists, Jews, and Muslims were "them." Of course, we Christians would never admit this, but we would organize our lives around avoiding "them." "We" excluded "them," and "they" excluded "us." We all thought the world would be a better place if there were more of "us" and less of "them."

I had been around other people, of course, but I did not *live* with them. Not really. Surely, I appeared to others and to myself as taking this exclusion in stride, but over time, their rejection turned into my rejection and into a massive contraction of my world and, as I later realized, of my heart.

We all thought the world would be a better place if there were more of "us" and less of "them."

The tables of judgment merely turned around. "Who can trust someone who would, when the moment of decision comes, trust something as limited and as self-serving as one's own reason?" we Christians wondered, shaking our heads.

After ten years, it finally dawned on me that I had no close non-Christian friends left! I had merely switched sides! This was a painfully humiliating realization. The incision from that divine splinter grew into a dangerous inflammation as I realized that isolated life, no matter which side one is on, was *not* an eternal kind of life.

SIBLINGS

The Hebrew words that speak of God and humans as compassionate have a root word *rekhem*, which means "womb." The Arabic cognate *rahim* is the root of the two most frequently used names for God, "the Compassionate" and "the Merciful," with which every chapter of the Quran except one begins. So when the Bible and Quran characterize God as "compassionate," they call up imagery that is as humanly understandable as possible. More literally, they say that God is "like a womb." As a woman feels compassion for the child who comes from her womb, so God has great compassion for us. As a child feels compassion for a sibling because they both come from the same womb, so every human being should have compassion for every other human being.

When God's water broke, we all came out together.

When the prophets said, "God is the God of all nations!" they were pleading, saying, as it were, "Don't we come from one womb? Isn't every life our life? Isn't every suffering our suffering?"

Your loss is not just your loss, and my loss is not just mine. It's not just Croatian for me and American for you. It's not just American for me and Asian for you. Not just Christian for me and atheist for you, Muslim for me and Hindu for you.

According to the Bible and the Quran, God is *womblike*. To bow before One God means to discover the compassion we carry inside ourselves. Whatever our beliefs about origins—whether God created us or whether we all came by chance out of some primordial soup—we all come from the same place and are therefore all siblings.

> *"They" are, in fact, "us."*

Our common origin precedes and therefore supersedes all other identities. As in a family, no matter how difficult it can be to live together, and no matter how dysfunctional the relationships can be, nothing can really separate us from each other. "They" are, in fact, "us."

IS GOD ENOUGH?

The Bible begins with a story of the creation of the world in which humanity is described in pristine innocence, harmony, and beauty. Curiously, though, at the end of the initial creation period, God declared it all "very good" *and* Adam as "troubled." In a perfect world, Adam was lonely and incomplete.

God was not enough.

That's how God wanted it. God created us in a way that we, like Adam, would not be satisfied just with God. According to the creation story, God created a universe in which we need someone other than God to satisfy our needs. God made us in such a way that we need each other to live abundantly in our world.

This need for *the other* was part of Adam's perfection. It demonstrated Adam's wholeness, not his brokenness.

Without the other, we cannot be well. Without yearning for the other, we are not whole.

When I arrived in the United States in the 1990s, I heard over and over again, in literature, education, and the media, that "in America, you can be whatever you want to be." This open-ended possibility was attractive and energizing and encouraged citizens to believe that each one of us could take action to control our own destinies. Wonderful, I thought. So I took advantage of it and resolved to make it in America. At the same time, being whatever I wanted to be felt like turning my back on something sacred, something that is good but not American, at least as defined by those propagating the slogan.

Do I really want to be all *I* want to be? Say, as a mental exercise, that I want to be a great architect. Obviously, my dream would involve the lives and dreams of other people. It includes those who clean my office, wash dishes in restaurants where I work with other architects, dig the foundations and create the space for my buildings—just to mention a tiny fraction of the people and details that my dream requires. For my dream to come true, there must be people who will dream of being janitors, dish washers, and construction workers. If they don't dream of those roles (or at least accept them), then someone's dream can't come true. Our individual dreams are inextricably connected with the lives of other people, starting with our own family members and extending all the way to people at the other end of the world.

We do not live in individual parallel universes. We live in the Kingdom of God, one world, on one finite and integrated planet, where "it is all about me" plus "it is all about all of us." I am to be concerned about the well-being of janitors, dish washers, and construction workers whom I need to assist me in becoming an architect. It is also about them.

I teach my young daughters that according to the scriptural account of humanity, the Kingdom of God is not about God at all—or at least our version of God. God does not need worshipers to heal God's wounded ego. It is we who have made God into a praise-hungry, love-hoarding, celestial self-centered being resembling ourselves. In contrast, God's compassion and God's dream, if one reads our religious texts more deeply, is for us first to acknowledge our common origins and common destiny. God created humanity to achieve community. In this sense, believing in and living for God means believing in and living for one another.

If I pursue whatever it is I want to be, then my family, my neighborhood, my city, my country, and ultimately humanity will be burdened instead of blessed by my dream. But if I pursue whatever *we* want to be, there's a chance for the world. This being together, of course, is not easy or may even be impossible to achieve. Yet imagination does count. Until more people start to claim their freedom to imagine the future of human society that is posttheocratic, postcommunist, and—this is the hard part in today's world, where we see human beings as *Homo economicus*—postcapitalist, we, along with our planet, will continue to drift toward self-destruction. The present prevailing vision is that the collective work of selfish individuals is the way to world harmony. This vision has expired.

Post- does not mean *anti-*. It means that something that used to work and brought us so far is not working anymore and that for our lives on this planet to continue, something new is going to be born, something that will demote "me" a notch or two and introduce the well-being of "us" and then demote "us" a notch or two and introduce the well-being of "them" as a path to abundant life.

> *Merely taking care of our own kind would ultimately not strengthen our own kind but diminish us all.*

At the time when I was expelled from home, my aunt Zuhra was the only person that stood up to my dad and regularly invited me to her home for a respite over a weekend, allowing me some peace of mind and putting my favorite food on the table. She taught me as a little boy that as a follower of Islam, I would have to learn to be "one who submits" (which is the literal meaning of the word *Muslim*). It has been taking me a lifetime to get over my visceral negative reaction to that terribly stifling concept of submission and understand that human submission is the reason why we are alive and well living together. Looking back, we were alive and well because of submission of her dreams to me, her nephew, and my dreams to her, my aunt, and submission of every human being to the well-being of their family members, friends, strangers, and enemies.

Later, as a Christian, remembering my aunt's words helped me understand that Jesus' commandments to love God and to love others are actually one. Love is one. Submission is one. Whatever separates us from one another is what separates us from God. Whatever brings us to one another brings us to God.

The ancient Scriptures provide a ground from which to look at our present situation in a critical way. Thousands of years of faith and wisdom tell us that instead of retreating into our own lot, our religious imagination can send us to the edges of our identity, to our boundaries, where we can, paradoxically, get closer to who we really are. Merely taking care of our own kind would ultimately not strengthen our own kind but diminish us all.

To *be* is to belong to one another. Can Judaism, Christianity, and Islam each be renewed to let God be the God of all humanity? If each can turn to its own history, texts, and traditions and dig deeper than ever before into this theme, change can come. If we get deep enough, we will hit the bottom of the wells of our religious traditions and rediscover a God who does not favor any particular "us."

UNIQUE BUT NOT APART

Recently, I visited Romemu, a Jewish congregation on the Upper West Side of Manhattan, led by Rabbi David Ingber. The Friday night service, related to the holiday of Purim that weekend, took place in a rented gym, with one wall of windows, many of them open. During the part of the service when we all turned toward

Jerusalem (with our backs to the windows) and were quietly vocalizing a Hebrew melody of longing and hope, a voice singing in the dark outside interrupted us. The distraction made us a bit nervous.

The strong, warm female voice seemed to be singing in Spanish to a melody that could be from South America or the Middle East. As her voice filled the dark city street and entered the gym to overpower ours, Rabbi David decided to embrace the moment and said, "Let's sing with her." So we did. We all started improvising together as one voice and wove our Hebrew melody into her song. Someone from the congregation interrupted the rabbi, shouting, "Everyone, come to the window!" We all turned around, and soon all of us were pressing closer to the windows to see what turned out to be a surprise.

Right below us was a Christian Easter procession, with fourteen large black-and-white art pieces depicting the traditional stations of the cross and fourteen young men dressed in white robes trailing a priest carrying a cross. Hundreds of followers of Jesus from Spanish Harlem stood in front of the building, absorbed in their song. The Jews started waving their hands above their heads, a motion of blessing, some of them grabbing their yarmulkes and lifting them up. Then people from the procession looked up to the large wall of windows and saw the silhouettes of the happily waving Jewish throng. Christians waved back. Everyone was momentarily confused about what had just happened. Holy awkwardness. But soon we could not stop smiling.

And that made me think: once we understand that we do belong to each other, what will happen to our differences? If "they" are, in fact, "us," wouldn't our boundaries disappear? Wouldn't beautiful but diverse songs of our religions melt into one?

Yale University theologian Miroslav Volf explains how boundaries between individuals and groups are a part of what it means to exist. God has created boundaries between soil, water, and air, between male and female, between light and dark, and in countless other ways. Irrespective of whether the world came into existence in short order or in billions of years, with or without God, existence requires boundaries.

> If "they" are, in fact, "us," wouldn't our boundaries disappear? Wouldn't beautiful but diverse songs of our religions melt into one?

Without boundaries, there would be jumbled chaos. Volf writes, "The absence of boundaries creates non-order, and non-order is not the end of exclusion but the end of life.... Vilify all boundaries, pronounce every discrete identity oppressive, put the tag 'exclusion' on every stable difference—and you will have aimless drifting instead of clear-sighted agency, haphazard activity instead of moral engagement and accountability and, in the long run, a torpor of death instead of a dance of freedom."[1]

Our differences are life-giving. They are not a matter of circumstances but a matter of principle. If reality is relational, differentiation is a blessing.

At the same time, we are all one. Volf asks, "Who are we? We are people with inclusive and changing identities; multiple others are part of who we are. We can try to eject them from ourselves in order to craft for ourselves an exclusive identity, but we will then do violence, both to others and to ourselves. Who is the other?...Others are not just others. They, too, have complex and dynamic identities, of which we are part, if we are their neighbors. Just as we are 'inhabited' by others and have a history with them, others are also 'inhabited' by us."[2]

Our otherness is not an absolute dimension of our being, not physically (our very lives depend on others), intellectually (we cannot know without being known), or spiritually (none of us can possess all that is sacred). We are all part of a larger web of life in which *the other* is part of our very own life.

We are all unique.

But not apart.

Looking back at my life story, I realize now that each of the worlds of which I was part regarded itself as not just different but "apart." We all saw our boundaries as something that *separate* us.

Like walls.

When I ask people to close their eyes and imagine boundaries, most people tend to imagine just that, walls.

Why walls?

Why not windows?

Why not doors?

Why not bridges?

They are boundaries too, aren't they?

GENESIS OF OUTSIDERS

We look at others and say, "We are insiders with God, and God is an insider with us. We are right and in, and they are wrong and out." We thus keep God in our servitude, in a cage built of words, meanings, and the teachings of our religion. Inevitably, our God then turns into a nongod and our religion into a self-serving ideology. But a God who can be enclosed by our religion is not worth worshiping.

> *Everyone fears some individuals or groups and blames them for whatever is wrong with the cosmic order.*

Without embracing the world as our community, the only difference between liberals and conservatives, believers and nonbelievers, Muslims and Jews, Christians and atheists is where we divide the world and whom we consciously or subconsciously vilify. Once we divide the world into insiders who "get it" (a good thing) and outsiders who "don't get it" (a bad thing), the purpose of life becomes oh, so obvious! Our life work then is to decrease the bad and increase the good in the world. The more people we get over the wall into our quarters, the better off the world will be!

Even those who say, "I am not religious at all," are still dividing the world. Everyone fears some individuals or groups and blames them for whatever is wrong with the cosmic order. Anti-Semites have used Jews. Jews have used Amalekites. Christians and Muslims have used pagans and one another. Atheists have used Christians. Protestants have used Catholics. Hutus have used Tutsis. Whites have used blacks. Communists have used capitalists. The rich have used the poor. On top of that, as Miroslav Volf convincingly and disturbingly argues, every group that was once a victim in turn becomes a perpetrator in some way. Sooner or later, all who have been excluded will in turn feign their complete innocence, not only of their past but also of their unwillingness to make steps toward healing.[3]

Religions, at their best, argue that our desire for exclusive "inner rings" are actually misplaced yearnings of all of us to belong. As long as we ourselves feel excluded, we will keep on excluding the other. C. S. Lewis once said that as long as you are governed by this desire to be in the inner ring, "you will never ever get what you want. You are trying to peel an onion: if you succeed there will be nothing left. Until you conquer the fear of being an outsider, an outsider you will remain!"[4]

A TIPPING POINT

When God called on Abraham, the father of Christians, Muslims, and Jews, God invited him to step outside. Out of his place, out of his people, out of what he had known about the world. God said, "Leave your country, your people, and your father's household...and I will bless you...and you will be a blessing...and all peoples on earth will be blessed through you."[5] In other words, "I want to bless the world. Would you be willing to receive the blessing and pass it on?" Abraham's faith was to be measured by the blessings it brings to outsiders. The blessing was instrumental. *He* was not blessed. He was blessed to be a blessing.

But there is more.

Abraham and his descendants were called to bless others the way God blessed them and therefore to allow them, the other, to be a blessing. Without this understanding, I doubt I would ever stay a Christian or subscribe to any version of monotheism. I became a Christian because I learned how much God loves me and how much I have to offer to the world. But that is not why I remain a Christian. The blessing given to me—being loved by God and having an opportunity to make a difference in the world—was not enough to keep my faith intact. It was the blessing that was given to *the other* that made me stay: God loves them, and they are blessed in order to be a blessing for me. God blesses every life.

I was invited to receive.

There is a difference between taking and receiving. Taking makes us strong. Receiving makes us weak. It is holy weakness, though.

We are called to learn not only how to bless "them" but also how to be blessed by "them," thus allowing other religions to thrive in doing good as a part of an interdependent world. The religions that will thrive in the future will be those that learn to measure success not only by how much they give to their adherents or by how much they bless nonadherents but by how much blessing they can receive from nonadherents.

And this is a tipping point.

Ever since I became a Christian, I have been taught to give.

That's what I was told over and over again, and it's what I taught others as a pastor, all the time. From my early days as a convert all the way to the halls of the theological seminary and then on to my work as a pastor in the city, I have been hearing and telling others, "In your school, love people. In your neighborhood, love people. In your workplace, love people." We call each other to minister to others, and that ministry always means serving others, caring for their needs, teaching them what they need to know. Giving, giving, giving to them. Blessing, blessing, blessing them. Loving, loving, loving them.

Since we have been teaching and acting in our Christian churches to love others and to organize our lives to love others, how curious, I thought, that polls report that non-Christians perceive Christians as *not loving*! How can that possibly be?

After adopting a practice of regularly stepping out of my evangelical religion and its meanings to look at them from the outside, here is what I have noticed. By and large, we don't really love because we don't know how to receive. We may love enough to take some help others have to offer in terms of material possessions, compliments, and friendships, but we are not willing to let them teach us anything about God, goodness, and grace—the stuff that really matters. Yes, we receive their kindness in a spirit of thankfulness, but in matters of God, we think they have nothing to add to our search for the eternal kind of life. In our minds, we are givers and they are receivers. And this is not just true of Christians.

We give because givers are in control.

We bless because blessers are in charge.

To receive, on the other hand, means to lose something. Gifts inevitably change relationships. As the Eskimos say hyperbolically, "Gifts make slaves." The recipient is usually perceived as the weaker party in the transaction and can become obligated and lose independence. Giving, in contrast, keeps us in control, subtly communicating the superiority of our worldview. Since our religion or worldview is an expression of what we consider true, valuable, and beautiful, holding the meaning of our lives together, accepting a gift from the other feels somehow like losing face, control, power, or value. We think it exposes the weakness or neediness in our group, casting us as lesser, dependent, or incomplete in our relationship with the other.

To be helpful, loving, and caring is thus an "imperial privilege" of religion that sees itself as self-sufficient on earth. Yes, we have learned to tolerate one another to some extent; Jews, Christians, Muslims, and atheists have learned to live parallel lives. But to achieve a human community, we must learn to *appreciate* what others have and at times receive and, yes, depend on what they have to give us.

In the relationship between religions, the attitude of being a sole dispenser of the ultimate blessing becomes not only irrational and arrogant but crushingly counterproductive. Everyone wants to teach, and nobody wants to learn! Everyone wants to stay in power by giving, and nobody wants to seem weak by receiving. That's why religions don't know how to repent of their historical failures, usually taking half a century to get around to it, if ever. Repentance means one needs to receive forgiveness, embrace holy weakness, and stop pretending to be above the frailties of human existence.

It is in the act of receiving that we concede God's presence in *the other*.

That's why evangelism in Christianity—sharing the good news—can nowadays only be done by a mature soul, one that knows how to receive in humility. Sharing of the good news is first and foremost a process of receiving the good news not as a once-in-a-lifetime event but as a way of life. We are to approach others by saying, "What I don't know about God, goodness, and grace, this person might."

> *Repentance means one needs to receive forgiveness, embrace holy weakness, and stop pretending to be above the frailties of human existence.*

I have come to believe that the world will need Christians once Christians learn to need the world. And this is not limited to Christians. One can substitute any identity in place of Christians.

By receiving a blessing from the other, we become partners with God. Each time we receive, we complete one circle of blessing that God began with them.

It is by receiving that we give.

EVERYTHING IS LIKE THE OCEAN

Fear of depending on the other paralyzes us. Those who fear cannot love, and those who cannot love cannot receive. The chain of blessing breaks, and the spiral of self-sufficiency takes us all down. The world where we each could live parallel lives, with wars to maintain the boundaries—that world is over. There are no more wars we can win. We are back to where we were at the beginning. The world today is like a womb where our lives are entangled with one another.

To alleviate suffering in a remote corner of the world or in a remote time in the future is thus not an act of charity anymore but an act of solidarity.

We are stuck together here on this shrinking planet, whether we like it or not, and this reality dawns on us every time we leave our isolated religious or ideological circles and venture out onto our streets. There are more and more of *the other* in our midst. Most of us literally have someone else living in our family, or will have soon, when our child or grandchild marries. No father like me can say anymore that a Muslim woman's son will not marry my daughter or that a Jewish man will not be her high school teacher or that an atheist will not help me find a job to feed my daughter in the first place.

Moreover, people on other continents are not merely the other, a faceless crowd "over there." They are *our other*, members of our extended family even though there is an ocean between us.

People who lived before us and will live after us are connected to us as well. Everything we do is linked to our past, and everything we achieve will be left in the hands of those who will come after us. To alleviate suffering in a remote corner of the world or in a remote time in the future is thus not an act of charity anymore but an act of solidarity.

As Father Zossima, a wise and revered elder of a monastery in Dostoyevsky's novel *The Brothers Karamazov*, says, "Everything is like the ocean, all things flow and are indirectly linked together and if you push here, something will move at the other end of the world.... If you push here, something somewhere will move; if you strike here, something somewhere will wince; if you sin here, something somewhere will suffer."[6]

Those who will be hurt or blessed by our thoughts, prayers, or actions might be completely unknown to us, but our lives *will* affect them, and their lives *will* affect us. Whatever we do, say, pray, or think, now matters to "them." Today, more than ever before, our share of life of the world is intertwined with everyone else's. As Kuan Tao-Sheng expresses it:

> *Take a lump of clay,*
> *Wet it, pat it,*
> *Make a statue of you*
> *And a statue of me*
> *Then shatter them, clatter them,*
> *Add some water,*
> *And break them and mold them*
> *Into a statue of you*

And a statue of me.

Then in mine, there are bits of you

And in you there are bits of me.

Nothing ever shall keep us apart.[7]

LOVING GOD WITH ALL OF MY LOVE

In 2005, a massive earthquake struck Pakistan, causing one of the greatest humanitarian disasters in modern history. Thousands were killed or injured, and millions were left homeless. Bob Simon of *60 Minutes* went to Kashmir to report on thirteen paramedics from New York who, at a time when the world was apathetic and failing to respond, dropped everything and flew to the area to help for an extended period of time.

Two worlds met.

There were huge barriers between them: culture, religion, race, language. "Them" met "them." Since there were no words to communicate, they used drawings and hand gestures. People in Kashmir did not know how to say things like "thank you" to these people who were completely other. And the other did not know how to say, "No. Thank *you*."

So a Pakistani man raised his hands in front of one of the paramedics. "Look, I have two hands."

Then he opened his palms wide. "Look, I have five fingers on each hand."

He then concluded, "You have two hands. You have five fingers on each hand."

"Human. I am human. Human. You are human," the man said beaming with joy.

This human life has everything to do with the divine. My deadpan honest and brilliant New York City friend Norm Buggel once raised his hand during the worship service discussion time and blurted out, "I can't love God." What flashed through my mind is that Norm would rarely, if ever, say, "I love God." It was just not something you could hear coming from him. He was one of those people who are usually absent from discussions of theology because they are impatient with words and are busy embodying them. Every gathering has people who for some reason do not fit in the group because they are not up to par in some way. They look like they don't have a clue, or taste, or a shower. Norm could always be found talking with these people, lavishing on them genuine curiosity and an open heart.

"If I can love God through loving people and the world, then I can love God with all of my love."

So when he said, "I can't love God," we all gave him space to explain himself, perhaps to confess that this whole God thing has been overrated. He continued, "I have so many people I am committed to love, but my time and resources are finite. If I add God to the list, I will only be able to give God a small part. But," Norm paused to try to find the right words to explain his silly sacrilegious confession and then continued tentatively, as if asking for permission, "if I can love God through loving people and the world, then I can love God with all of my love."

At that moment, I came to understand how sweet and real Norm's love for God really was. Norm isn't about God because God isn't about God. Or alternatively, Norm is all about God because to be all about God is to be all about all of us.

God lives out his life through each of us. To love anyone is to love God too. To hurt anyone is to hurt God too. That's why the early history of monotheistic religions is significant. Our beginnings provided embodiments of this truth. The Jewish nation was called out of Egypt to forge a new kind of society that would bless others by pursuing justice, peace, and the beauty of the human experience. Christianity began as an extraordinary community of people who loved the downtrodden and downcast, giving their own lives in the process. And when the Prophet Muhammad founded his first community in Medina, he and his followers made sure to respond to the time and place with a radical individual and social transformation toward justice, equality, and human rights. Theirs, like Israel and the early church, was a "community on earth."[8] At our beginnings, our communities had their heart in heaven and their feet firmly planted on the ground.

We can't simply "love God."

What keeps us from one another keeps us from God.

What connects us to one another connects us with God.

God is about the other, and until we embrace the other, we will never fulfill our own devotion to God.

MY SECOND PRAYER

My first prayer changed my life. I uttered it on that bench in the army camp when I realized that God loved me. I simply said, "God," and my world changed forever.

Another life-changing prayer came at a worship service in a Christian church in New York City. This congregation's way of interpreting the Bible and its approach to theology were different from mine. It was a struggle for me. I picked up an attitude along the way that those who disagree with the view of Christianity espoused by my own church are wrong and have to be corrected. And it was my duty to do so! We were taught that in the matters of the gospel, we are to be the teachers and other Christians are to be the learners. So whenever I went to another church, I would feel oppressed by my own anxieties about the orthodoxy I felt I was called to defend.

> *A that moment, a decade's worth of words of defending my brand of religion were loosened and fell from my shoulders. Silly me! How could I ever have excluded people like this?*

But in this particular church, on this particular Sunday, the Beloved visited me again. The service was not unusual. People sang Christian hymns with passion and confidence. Tired of my worry about orthodoxy, my heart drifted to the songs people were singing. I felt compelled to sing with them. Not just sing along, but sing as though God loves my very bad voice! An unmistakable wave of gratitude washed over me as I realized that no matter how different these people might be, they were my brothers and sisters—God's gift to me. At that moment, a decade's worth of words of defending my brand of religion were loosened and fell from my shoulders. Silly me! How could I ever have excluded people like this? I felt like hugging and kissing these unsuspecting people, like the night when Faith first kissed me.

Suddenly, I felt compelled to leave.

Pulled gently by the invisible hand of my Beloved, I walked out briskly, away from the church to a busy Manhattan intersection with a pedestrian island in the middle. In the midst of a crowd of people, I looked up to the sky through the space between the tall buildings and said the second prayer that forever changed my life: "Our God." And that was it.

"Our."

Saying this word, I admitted that God is not only "my" God. That neither I nor my church nor Christianity is in charge of God.

"Our."

In my mind I see a Mongolian family standing in front of their nomadic tent, a photograph I saw in *National Geographic*. I look at the father's crooked legs, his wife's dark hair, the faces of two small children. They are all looking back at me.

I picture an imam I have never met, with a big beard, who lives somewhere in my city, serving in a mosque perhaps walking distance from my home. His kind hand is touching my shoulder.

I imagine a teacher in a public elementary school, a dedicated Buddhist. She is pouring out her best efforts, day in and day out, as she meditates to keep herself well, teaching my daughter about what matters in life.

When I pray the Lord's Prayer, I see all of them standing around me.

I begin the prayer that Jesus taught us: "Our Father..."

Who is included in this word "our"?

After that first prayer when I said, "God," there was no way back to unbelief. God was there to stay in my life. After this prayer when I said, "Our God," there was no way back to unbelief either. *The other* was here to stay in my life.

EPILOGUE

MY STORY AND MAYBE YOURS

While I was serving as a pastor at CrossWalk, a creative and loving church community in Southern California, my parents and my sister came from Croatia to visit. They had been to the United States before, and we had visited them in Croatia, but this trip turned out to be quite unlike the others. After twenty years, my family was finally going to visit my Christian world.

Our days were filled mostly with cooking. As the three of them took over our spacious American kitchen, the aroma of wholesome food brought back memories of the time when we were one of the happiest families on earth.

One Sunday afternoon, as I watched my mom put a delicious cherry strudel into the oven, I thought that she looked old and worn out by life. But her eyes seemed happier than ever. It seemed her heart had grown, through the past twenty years of our family's struggle. She had turned pain into blessings and dispensed them to the family. Someone told me that "grace knows how to overlook." My mom was full of grace that way, overlooking my dad's and my own inexcusably self-absorbed behavior over the years. What would have happened to us if it weren't for her?

Looking out the window of our living room, I saw my dad, an unstoppable force in our family for half a century, patiently painting our porch. Everything he attempted, he did with integrity and joy, mixed with lots of good food. Where would I be without him? How could I have learned to love life so fervently without his passion burning before me and his integrity inspiring me?

While my mom and dad were busy with their self-selected chores, my sister, Bisera, lay down on the sofa and took a nap. I looked at her aging body. For two decades, she had cared for our parents as they anguished over me, and at the same time raised her own beautiful family. My sister has been a spring of laughter and common sense in our family. I thought, "She deserves a long, sweet nap. How would we ever have stayed together without her stamina?" I wanted my daughters to grow up to be like her.

During the four weeks of their visit, we talked about everything— except faith. We had learned to pretend that religion could be left in a back room, like a locked up monster, best left undisturbed. Each weekend during their visit, my wife, our two daughters, and I would go to church, and the three of them would stay at home. And while we were at church, we were thinking of them and they were thinking of us.

Then I thought of the day twenty years earlier when I walked into my father's office to tell him for the first time about my faith in God. And it came to me, why not do the same thing again? Only this time, I can invite my dad into *my* office. And I did. As soon as he walked into my home office, where we were alone, I said, "Would you like to come and visit my church and see what I do?"

My dad turned to the window.

"You know how I feel about that," he said. "I can't get over it."

"You don't have to get over it," I replied.

"I don't want anyone to think that I approve of your religion," he said.

"This is not about our religious convictions. This is because I'm asking you. Because I love you and you love me. I want you to see what my life is about." I knew this could well be the last trip my parents would make to this side of the globe, so I added, "You're getting old, Dad. This might be the last chance for you to see my world from within."

After a pause, he said, "All right," and quietly walked out of my office, still visibly shaken after all these years.

In the living room, my mom and sister anxiously waited for him. Both of them were on board with my plan, murmuring their religionless prayers for me and my dad. We brokered a more detailed agreement over the next couple of days. They would come to the worship service, but not for the music, just for "the lecture." They could not let the word "sermon" pass their lips. For them, it was not a normal word.

The next weekend was a high weekend for my church, and it was packed with seven hundred people. The deacons kept seats reserved for my family's late arrival to hear "the lecture." As the praise music wound down, they arrived. My sister and my wife translated into Croatian for my mom and dad. I titled my sermon simply "Love."

After greeting the congregation, I began: "Here is my first and most direct experience of love." An old black-and-white wedding picture of my mom and dad was projected on the large screens in the auditorium. Next came a close-up of their faces beaming with love for each other. I went through their honeymoon in a series of pictures, including some they took in a photo booth, kissing, caressing, laughing, feeding their hearts by looking into each other's eyes.

"That's love," I said.

"And guess who this is." The picture showed a small boy in overalls sitting on the front steps of a project apartment building. It was little Samir, eyes beaming, full of wonder and joy.

"Because my mom and dad loved each other, I exist."

Then I went through some snapshots of my life, including one where I sported the broad grin of someone who could quote the Bible on any topic, stop and police any conversation that was not about God—the grin of one of the ardent defenders of God on earth. "This is when I became a Christian," I continued. "My parents couldn't understand how this could have happened to them. I considered becoming a follower of Jesus the greatest thing that had happened to me. They saw it as the greatest disappointment of their lives." I gave a short history of their attempts to "win me back to sanity" and then continued:

> They tried everything possible to bring me back to my senses, and after they had exhausted all they could do, they decided to go for the last resort and expel me from home. They did it with the hope that difficulties would teach me something and bring me back to them.

> But after two years of separation, they couldn't take it anymore, so they lovingly brought me back and learned to live with me.

> When I became a Christian, my mom, my dad, and my sister were hurt beyond what I can describe with words or perhaps will ever be able to understand, but they loved me through it.

> And they are here today, in what to them is a very strange place. They have stepped into a church for the first time in their lives and in my twenty years as a Christian. And this may be the only time they will ever be here.

> There are people who must endure our conversions and the best intentions of our religions. There are millions of unsung heroes of God like my parents. Even Jesus respectfully and

compassionately acknowledged how difficult a response to his call might be for family members. So please, do me a favor, all of you, and give them a standing ovation for the love they have shown me despite the fact I became something they could not understand. That would mean a lot to me.

Everyone stood up and offered a heartfelt *thank-you*: long, loud, sincere. I felt God's healing hand lifting us up. I relished every second of it. Then I said, "Mom, Dad, Sister, thank you for your love. Everything good that I am, and everything good that I have, is because of you and your love for me."

I was proud of my church.

I was proud of my family.

At that moment, for the first time, I belonged to my family *and* to my church.

We never belong to a religion anyway. We always belong to people. Even our belonging to God is experienced through people.

After the worship service, my mom beamed, her face and body filled with a fresh supply of energy that will last her for years to come; my sister felt peace, knowing that her burden of keeping us together had borne fruit; and my dad awkwardly tried to stay in control of his good vibes, joking that my "lecture" went on and on for forty minutes.

I have no doubt that my decision to follow Jesus was a direct result of my parents' love for each other and their love for me. When

I first read the ancient Scriptures and saw the way the prophets and poets of old loved and suffered for their people; the way Jesus approached, treated, and suffered with people; and the way good came out of it all, I got Jesus. Because of my parents, I knew love when I saw it. When Jesus said in John 14, "I am the way and the truth and the life,"[1] I believed him. They were my best witnesses of Christ's way, truth, and life—my first evangelists.

That day at church, we all received grace from above and experienced a new beginning.

> *It felt as if God had stopped time, just for me, so that I could become intoxicated with the love of God.*

As the church people walked toward their cars in the parking lot, they stopped to greet my parents and chat, some attempting to say a word or two in Croatian, just to make them even happier. It felt as if God had stopped time, just for me, so that I could become intoxicated with the love of God. I had been waiting two decades for this—for my church to treat my family as human beings and for my family to treat my church members as human beings. One world. The Kingdom of God was right there, exactly the way Jesus described it.

THE WHIRLWIND THAT NEVER STOPS

We must have a conversation about religion. A broad, deep, and long conversation. Each religion—which, to repeat, includes any system of meaning—with all of humanity, that is, with our entire ethical community. We cannot simply claim "our God" as "our judge." Our religions and other systems are all in this same boat the size of a planet. Our destiny is so intertwined that none of us can say, "Please leave me alone; I am drilling the boat floor under *my* seat and not yours. I live my way, and you live yours." Now we all travel or sink together. Life is never simply ours. God, good, and grace are always present in the other as well, and the transformation begins when we touch the bottom of our religions and find life that includes others. We realize what should be obvious: the Kingdom of God is God's, not ours.

Another word for the Kingdom of God that Jesus talked about is "reality." Instead of saying, "The Kingdom of God is here," Jesus could just as well have said, "The Kingdom of God is the way things are." That's why honesty about our religion can't hurt us. It can heal us. Life's proof is penicillin for our religious illusions. And nobody can help us see life's proof like strangers.

My family and my church were strangers to each other.

The stranger is different from us. The stranger is in the image of God—God's *Tzelem*. Both.

The solutions we cannot find and the blessings we cannot receive are out of our reach precisely because they are where we "know" they are not! Not in what we already know but precisely in what we don't. Not in what we think but in what we don't. The stranger, like an uninvited celestial consultant, can see what we cannot or refuse to see. The stranger reveals.

And that's the problem of a stranger. To survive, we need to protect ourselves from the stranger; to survive, we need the stranger to help us see.

In Scripture, the problem of a stranger has been inverted and transformed into one of the most potent commandments for the faithful. While the Hebrew Bible commands "You shall love your neighbor" only once, it commands no less than thirty-six times that we "love the stranger," as in Leviticus 19: "When an alien lives with you in your land, do not mistreat him. The alien living with you must be treated as one of your native-born. Love him as yourself."[2] In the New Testament, Jesus insists that the ultimate judgment of our acts will come from the way we treat the stranger because the stranger stands for none else than Jesus.[3] In the Muslim world informed by the Quranic texts, one is expected to take strangers into one's home, treat them with honor, and care for them no less than three days, even when these strangers are considered an enemy.

> *To survive, we need to protect ourselves from the stranger; to survive, we need the stranger to help us see.*

This may seem nothing but a simple invitation to the virtue of neighborly love, but there is far more to this insistent call of God. I have always wondered why the mysterious priest of the most high, Melchizedek, was summoned to bless the "first" believer, Abraham, and why wise men from the East (who were actually astrologers) were needed by God to confirm the identity of the newborn Jesus. Couldn't God use "our" people?

Understanding our relationship and life with the Divine Other—the Holy One who will always confound us—is inextricably intertwined with our relationship and life with the human other—humanity that also confounds us. The human other is a fractal or a trace of the Divine Other in whose image the stranger has been made. Without knowing and being known by strangers, we cannot grow in knowing either God or ourselves. And now globalization has turned our societies into wonderful societies of strangers where every religion has a fresh chance to transcend its own limitations! As Rabbi Brad Hirschfield testifies with the story of his life, we are now called to notice the person in front of us before the ideology inside of us and make choices to privilege that person.[4]

When the Mishnah (a collection of early oral interpretations of the Hebrew Scriptures) says that the world is like a thorny bush with one rose and that Israel is that rose and that other nations are the thorns, or when Jesus says that his name is the only one that can lead anyone to God and seems to imply that those who do not know Jesus are abandoned by God, or when the Quran says that infidels need to be destroyed, the meaning of these texts will change if they are read *in the presence* of the other. Literally. When the thorns, the abandoned, and the infidels are present, when their eyes look into ours, the life context of our interpretation will change and so will the interpretation of the text. Not just the tenor of it but its basic logic. When God visits us through *the other*, we are awakened and begin to feel what we could not feel before, we see what we could not see before, and we think what we could not think before. In the presence of *the other*, everything changes.[5]

The Golden Rule of treating others as you want to be treated is deeply embedded in all major religions.[6] Let's then imagine, as Karen Armstrong suggests, that we interpret the whole of our Scriptures as a commentary on the Golden Rule and read the whole of *their*—and I would add *our*—Scriptures with Augustine's rule of always seeking the most charitable interpretation of the text.[7] Not only would this reflect the best of our traditions, but paradoxically, it would work to preserve our own religions. To seek God means, among other things, to seek God *among* the other as we want the other to seek God among us.

Such *charitable* interpretations would also have to be complemented by *courageous* interpretations of the text through which we can enter into a dynamic relational tension with our own texts. As in a relationship with a person we love, our relationship with the text would also involve disagreement and conflict and, at times, apparent disobedience to the text. To contradict and disobey specific texts on the basis of the entire relationship with the entire text can be a way to honor our texts. Furthermore, to risk one's own standing in one's own religion and with one's own God for the sake of the well-being of *the other* might turn out to be a far deeper way to love one's own text and obey one's own God. This would require deepening of our identity. Jonathan Sacks, chief rabbi of England, writes: "The pursuit of peace can come to seem to be a kind of betrayal. It involves compromise. It means settling for less than we would like. It has none of the purity and clarity of war, in which the issues...are unambiguous and compelling. War speaks to our most fundamental sense of identity: there is an 'us' and a 'them' and no possibility of confusing the two. When, though, enemies shake hands, who is now 'us' and who the 'them'? Peace involves a profound crisis of identity."[8]

Relativity and passive tolerance will not withstand the fervor of those who are afraid of peace. As Rabbi Sacks points out, "Only an equal and opposite fervor can do that. Healing...must come, if anywhere, from the heart of the whirlwind itself."[9]

In the past, the whirlwind of religious passion came from our experiences of being visited, corrected, and blessed by God. Today, God has not withdrawn but is calling us to a profound experience of meeting God in the stranger as God's people did in the past. Religion has an exciting future. For those who are open to strangers, the whirlwind never stops.

MAKING THE SECRET PUBLIC

Meister Eckhart said that our religions are like houses. Each house has a trap door somewhere down in the basement, and if we go deep enough, we will fall through the trap door into a river that flows beneath all of us. Beautiful, I thought. But then I wondered, why not use the front door? Why is this truth of mutual belonging accessible only to those who hang out in the basement? Why do we need to be tricked into finding it?

Why neglect or hide this truth of common blessing? Why not celebrate it?

Humankind is like a living organism, a body in which religions are the various parts, in which diversity is a matter of life. Every part has a function that serves the other parts. As in biodiversity, our glory is not diminished but rather fulfilled in serving the well-being of the other. A kidney, no matter how large, cannot survive without being connected to other parts of the body, serving them and being served by them. We cannot function the way some people seem to want, undisturbed, separated from one another, a collection of organs in separate glass jars.

> *Humankind is like a living organism, a body in which religions are the various parts.*

What, ultimately, makes any religion thrive? When can we know that a religion is right and true to its own ideals, that it works? By its words? Rituals? Worship? Practices? Even if every single adherent to a religion "gets it" in every single way, it would still not be enough to show that the religion works! The promise of your religion and mine is not the well-being of religion but *the well-being of the world*. The earth, for example—the new poor and oppressed of the world—does not have a religion. Each religion has a job to do to save our earth, but it is a job we all share by the fact that we are all responsible for it together. The earth is suffering, and suffering unites humanity. Our bonds are mystical, but as Paul Knitter, a distinguished theologian of pluralism today, says, "mystical bonds are formed in ethical action."[10]

Interdependence is therefore not an elective activity or peripheral to our identity anymore. Too much is at stake to leave this work to those few who fall through the trap doors of our religions. The time has come for the secret of our oneness to go public! Our identity is now forged at the boundaries where our religion touches the world.

WHEN THE FUTURE SITS AT OUR TABLE

I talked to my daughters about religion as honestly and as openly as I knew how, expressing my worries and hopes to them. I told them that we need to bring our religions together not only in tolerance and dialogue but also in a way that will help everyone live interdependently.

One evening, we were driving home from an event that stirred these issues in their young heads. We had met Bono, lead singer of U2, at a private party in Los Angeles where he spoke about the Product Red Campaign to benefit the poorest areas of the world by sustaining their local economies. Our older daughter, Ena, gave him a poem she had written about the plight of Africa's fathers and mothers. Bono read it, complimented Ena for one particular line, kissed her, and then said in his cool Irish way that he would "keep the poem in the front pocket of his jacket, close to his heart, all the way to Dublin."

On the way home, Leta, then nine years old, piped up from the backseat, "I don't think these religions can ever live together. Dad, your idea won't work." When eleven-year-old Ena probed, Leta strenuously argued that Jews, Muslims, and Christians simply do not want to do it. "It's just too complicated," she said.

"People just want to do what they want to do. Everyone wants to be right." Neither my wife, at the wheel, nor I said anything right away. I found myself thinking, their eyes have already seen too much. Two of the most tender beings we know were discussing the hardest problem on earth.

They *have* to. It's their future that is at stake.

I wondered if archbishops, influential mullahs, chief rabbis, distinguished professors, powerful politicians, and leading economists could pull up a chair and invite the future to sit at the table, and perhaps keep an empty chair around the tables where decisions are made, a seat for my daughter, or yours.

Unfortunately, that is seldom the case. It seems that only the present, with its considerations focused tightly on the immediate state of economics, politics, and religion, is invited to sit at the table. Future generations are conspicuously absent from these discussions. We do not ask, "How will this decision affect people fifty or two hundred years from now?" In his book *Orthodoxy*, G. K. Chesterton made a convincing appeal for respect of tradition and the past instead of idolizing the present. It seems we are coming to a new milestone in our thinking where Chesterton's notion of a "democracy extended through time" has to extend into the future as well.[11]

Our locus of concern has narrowed to *today*, which is another way of saying "us." We have become self-centered and therefore ultimately self-destructive. And as I describe in the Introduction, our children are looking at us, their silence asking us, "What have you done?"

What if God sees and judges our religions through the eyes of children who will inherit the earth after we are gone? Why not hear the questions they will ask then? "Did those defenders of God listen to the poor?" "Did they feel the hurt of the other?" "Did they love the earth?" What would

> *What if we did religion not simply as Jewish, Christian, and Muslim sisters and brothers but as mothers and fathers?*

happen if we interpreted our sacred texts and traditions not in the quiet of our rooms, not in the glory of our temples, and not to preserve our past—in fact, not to prove anything at all? What would happen if we were to study, pray, and practice our faith under the gaze of each other's sons and daughters? What if we did religion not simply as Jewish, Christian, and Muslim sisters and brothers but as mothers and fathers?

LAUGHTER, TEARS, AND SPONTANEOUS UPHEAVAL

The morning after my parents visited my church world, earlier than usual, I went back to the church building. After parking the car, I walked through the empty parking lot where my family and I had stood the day before. The Spirit of God was still lingering there as a cold California desert night was about to yield to the heat of the rising sun. Feelings of joy about being visited by God and regret about a life wasted in strife over things religious swelled within me.

I had the urge to laugh.

About my religion.

So I did; I laughed there, alone in the parking lot. We humans laugh in response to incongruence. Laughter is one of the ways we cope with the discrepancies of our lives.[12] There is a dream we all have for this world, and then there is, well, this world. There are expectations we have of our religions, and then there are our religions.

And all of us—Muslims, Christians, Jews, atheists, Hindus, Buddhists, witches, everyone—can agree that there is incongruence between our deepest aspirations and our experiences. It is so sad, and it is also beautiful. And funny. The theologian Thomas Oden writes:

> We students of God, look at us: God's own image scratching our eczema; irritated by hemorrhoids, yet capable of the refracting divine goodness; biped animals who dream of eternity; playing God yet being bums, clowns, and louts—yet bums who can say from the heart "God bless"; clowns who mime the posture of Superman; louts who can conceive of the idea of perfect being. We are curious about divine judgment, but a little less so than about the brakes on our car; recipients of rationality who cannot balance our bank accounts; living souls puzzled by death. Such a creature it is who takes up pen and ink and scribbles vague sentences about God; who breathes polluted air and speaks of Spirit; who uses the name of God mostly to intensify cursing, yet who calls God the Adorner of Creation.[13]

I came to believe that our capacity to love God, ourselves, people, and all of life grows with our capacity to laugh. We are ridiculous, and not to laugh at our religions, our worldviews, and our philosophies (that is, ourselves) would be a false witness, would be a lie.

Laughter lets us take ourselves less seriously so that we can take God and God's world more seriously.

We constantly bumble between our dreams and dignity on the one hand and human realities on the other. And that's why laughing about our religions is far more than a sugarcoated pill, slapping a happy face on our mess. It is about more than purposeful living, positive thinking, the power of intention, or the law of abundance. It is a confession of hope. It is an act of faith.

This ability to laugh in the midst of our imperfections in the presence of God is what we call grace. It is all around us, and those who have eyes to see and ears to hear will see and hear—and touch it and smell it and taste it.

I am not talking here about ridiculing the religion of others or our own. Mocking is an act of exclusion; humor is an act of embrace. The wisdom that allows us to laugh about our religion is of Divine origin, an ever-present reminder of our creaturehood and an antidote to our unquestioning dependence on our God management systems. Laughter lets us take ourselves less seriously so that we can take God and God's world more seriously.

Standing in that parking lot, after laughing it out, I felt like crying.

So I cried. Years' worth of tears. I sat down on the curb next to my car and buried my face in my hands.

I wished I were not alone.

I wished others were with me. I needed someone to embrace me, someone who could forgive. Perhaps people who were harmed by my religion.

So we could grieve together. And lose our religions in order to find them.

Ever since, I have wished for some interfaith crying service where we could let go of our exceptionalism. We are quick to say, "Look at *their* history. Look at *their* actions. Look at *their* indifference. *They* have done so much injustice. *They* have spilled blood." But no matter to whom we apply the words "they" and "them," when we judge others, we judge ourselves. Not only can I not disown Christians who have killed in the name of God in centuries past—they are my spiritual ancestors, without whom I would not be a Christian—but I also cannot disown killing done by my Muslim or Jewish cousins because they are *my* people too. If we humans belong to one another, then our evil deeds also belong to one another. It is always *we* who have neglected, oppressed, and killed.

We have to ask God and humanity to forgive *us* for what *they* have done.

Tears would help us be honest. We would be able to admit that we all find conflicts useful. We perpetuate fear, violence, and stupidity for a reason. They help us sell everything from books to tanks. They help us stay in power, get away with crimes, solidify the commitments of our followers, and medicate the pain of our doubts. Patience, conversation, humility, service, and peace would simply be too costly for us. Our wars are not fought over God, truth, justice, or love but over land, resources, and power. This cannot be seen clearly but through our tears.

And tears can be held back for only so long. Thomas Merton writes about the spontaneous upheaval that will grip our world:

> We are living in the greatest revolution in history—a huge spontaneous upheaval of the entire human race: not the revolution planned and carried out by any particular party, race, or nation, but a deep elemental boiling over of all the inner contradictions that have ever been in man, a revelation of the chaotic forces inside everybody. This is not something we have chosen, nor is it something we are free to avoid.[14]

To have faith is to set one's heart on and forge a working relationship with a mystery. This can be done in a way that embraces the other or in a way that abandons the other.

Our diverse mysteries will remain, but the way we hold them can change.

We can hold our mysteries with more laughter about ourselves, more tears for the stranger, and more whirlwind for us all. We are better together.

And as upheavals come, may life win.

READER'S GUIDE

Ted Ewing

This book will be most nourishing if you enjoy it like a good meal—with others. Use the questions like silverware to sample the content and facilitate self-discovery, self-disclosure, and meaningful dialogue.

Gather to share stories, wrestle with the ideas presented by the author, and imagine personal responses.

Don't force-feed. Don't be intimidated by silence. Enjoy the meal and those sharing it with you.

PROLOGUE: LIFE WINS

1. The author writes, "For Soo and most of her friends, church was a treacherous place" (p. 1). If you have ever experienced a place like that, what were the circumstances, and how did the experience affect you?

2. The author calls the gift of diversity among us the "treasure of difference" (p. 12). What are some of the treasures of including people who are often excluded?

3. We usually think of uncertainty as a negative and certainty as a positive, but the author asserts, "Now I am looking for a better kind of certainty" (p. 6). When and how can uncertainty be beneficial and certainty harmful?

4. In an effort to increase his exposure to life beyond his own religion, the author "made it a personal discipline to take trips outside the boundaries of Christianity" (p. 8). What experiments or disciplines might you embrace to expose yourself to life beyond the boundaries of your system of meaning?

5. The author observes, "We find it difficult to accept that others have anything significant to teach us about what we hold sacred, about our God" (p. 17). Who are some of the others whose insights you have difficulty accepting, and what could you do to allow them to teach you?

CHAPTER 1: LIVING WITH A SPLINTER

1. Celtic Christians used the term *thin places* to describe sites where they experienced the sacred. The author suggests, "A thin place could be a conversation, a dream, a room, a tree, a dawn, a shore, a dance, a person, a scientific lab, a Sabbath, a Eucharist, an early morning meal before the Ramadan fast begins" (p. 24). What are some of your thin places, and what do you experience there?

2. What practices in the author's family of origin did you find most similar and most different from your own?

3. The author notes that in his family of origin, "there were two doctrines, unspoken, but as solid as any religious dogma can be. The first doctrine was called Pleasure: "Thou shalt enjoy life" (p. 30). "The second doctrine of our religion was Honor: 'Thou shalt not be a jerk'" (p. 32). What were some of the key doctrines of your own family of origin?

4. The author says, "We are terrified of the prospect of finding the image of God in those who are not in our image. But . . . let's each one of us begin to say this around our kitchen tables, religious meetings, coffee shops, town squares, and chat rooms: 'I am made in the image of God. I am made in God's *Tzelem*. We all are.' And then let us all tell our stories to each other" (p. 29). What aspects of God's image do you see revealed in someone you know?

5. What would the present chapter of your story be titled, and why?

CHAPTER 2: THE SECRET OF THE ORDINARY

1. In what ways do you experience "an unbroken chain of the sacred lacing the ordinary" (p. 49) on a fairly regular basis?

2. How have you and others segregated life and "shrunk the sacred" (p. 56) to exclude the ordinary and consequently diminish life?

3. Why and how did the ordinary lives of extraordinary figures such as Jesus seem to infuse meaning, purpose, and vitality into the ordinary?

4. What specific sacraments do you practice, and how might you use them as "gates" and not "enclosures" (p. 60) that restrict access to the temple of life?

5. Describing what he calls the Third Exodus, the author addresses Christians: "We can either stay within the Christianity we have mastered with the Jesus we have domesticated, or we can leave Christianity as a destination, embrace Christianity as a way of life, and then journey to reality, where God is present and living in every person, every human community, and all creation" (p. 63). How might you and your faith community experience a Third Exodus?

CHAPTER 3: GOD MANAGEMENT SYSTEMS

1. The author asks, "Have we turned our religious texts, traditions, and rituals into containers and dispensers of God?" (p. 69). He writes, "Quietly, over the ages, our religions have colonized the name of God and become God management systems" (p. 91). Have you found this to be true in your own experience of religion? If so, what has been the result?

2. The author says of certain Christians, "They can't live without Jesus, but they can't live with Christianity" (p. 68), and quoted his disappointed Jewish real estate broker: "I have only two pillars to my Jewishness: fear of another Holocaust

and fear of losing the land of Israel. These two are not enough to sustain a religion. I need a Judaism that goes deeper" (p. 83). He concludes, "People want God, but not one who is the captive of a religion. They want an unmanaged God" (p. 92). How would you describe what these people want?

3. The author describes organized religion as, "like everything else in the world, broken and beautiful, fallen and redeemable" (p. 68). In your experience, what are some things people gain and lose by participating in organized religion?

4. Toward the end of the chapter, the author cautions, "Religion is in trouble. If we cannot move beyond our 'all-encompassing' views of God, if we cannot hold something more sacred than our own understanding, if we cannot have a sense of creaturely self-doubt about the way we understand not only God but anything at all, we all have failed the world we are supposed to serve.... If there is nothing we can aspire to better than Christianity, Islam, Judaism, Hinduism, or atheism, a bloodbath then seems inevitable" (pp. 90–91). In your opinion, how did he arrive at such a grave warning?

5. The author ends on a positive note: "There is hope. There is a solution. And it is not to stop going to our churches, synagogues, mosques, temples, libraries, bars, and other places where our worldviews are shared, challenged, and affirmed. Our convictions need to be deepened, not watered down. Our communities need to be blessed, not abandoned.

The way out of this mess is being dug by people who are ready to live interdependently instead of self-sufficiently" (p. 91). What do you imagine it would take for this solution to be implemented in your circle of friends or faith community?

CHAPTER 4: WHY IS GOD NOT MORE OBVIOUS?

1. What is attractive to you about things that you consider mysterious? What about them do you find frustrating?

2. The author uses terms of intimacy to describe his encounter with God: "I walked back to the barracks without fully understanding anything of what I have just described. I just experienced it. Understanding came later. I felt moisture from the Beloved's lips still on my forehead, my heart and lungs pulsing in exhilaration, my hands embracing my own body, my eyes blinking through my tears, my face blushing under the stars. I wanted another kiss" (p. 98). Is this kind of language common among the members of your organization or faith community? Why or why not?

3. In discussing the limitations of words to convey human experience of the sacred, the author uses the analogy of music: "God's presence feels. Like music. . . . Music seeks a response. An embrace. A dance" (p. 103). What are things you could do regularly to transcend the language of your faith?

4. The author states, "Downplaying our religious histories, traditions, teachings, and practices only forfeits our opportunity to push back against the destructive force of the idolaters

of certainty. Their conviction cannot be countered by non-conviction but only by a passion stronger than theirs—the passion of a lover" (p. 117). In what healthy ways might you express your passion to "push back against the destructive force of the idolaters of certainty"?

5. The author finishes, "Sitting on a bench away from the army barracks between two worlds, my desire for certainty was not fulfilled. I left desiring another kiss. And that's why I remain a believer! My unfulfilled yearning for God is sweeter than any other desire ever fulfilled. My uncertainty with God is more comforting than any certainty I have ever known. I am held. And the kisses of the Beloved keep coming" (p. 121). Where is your bench, and how do the kisses come for you?

CHAPTER 5: WHERE DOES YOUR HEART GO?

1. The author proposes that we all exercise trust on a daily basis. "In our beds, we enter a zone of trust. . . . We leave everything in hands other than our own. We relinquish control. We release the clutch. We believe that in the not-too-distant future, we will wake up able to walk, talk, think, and feel all over again. We trust" (131–132). At what other times in the course of your day do you consciously or unconsciously exercise faith?

2. The author wonders if both religious and nonreligious people seek "to simplify and manage the otherwise unbearable complexity of human experience" (p. 134). What do your

current spiritual practices—for example, how you spend your time, energy, or money—reveal about how you seek to simplify and manage the complexity of human experience?

3. The author suggests that all people construct idols—religious and nonreligious—and warns against religion itself becoming an idol. "We need to be reminded again and again that religion is not the pearl but the shell that holds the pearl.... When we free our religion from the burden of being our God, we empower it. It begins to serve us and the world around us. Religions that will matter in the future will enable their adherents to live in tension with their own religiosity" (p. 142). How could you seek to live with this tension in your own family, friendships, or faith community?

4. The author reemphasizes the importance of the *other* when he explains, "we need religions other than our own. Other religions can challenge (or at least help us see) the idols we create because they expand the whole territory of knowing. They pose difficult questions we don't want to ask, make assumptions we don't want to acknowledge or examine, create meaningful arguments against us we don't want to consider, and expose harmful practices we don't want to stop" (p. 146). What might you, your family, or your friends do to express your need to other religious traditions?

5. The author extends an invitation to let your religion go and allow God to enter the spaces that are freed as a result. Obviously, this is a process involving repeated release. "As you lie on your bed tonight, may your heart, released from

the clutches on nongods, find rest in love that is better than life" (p. 149). What could you do over the next few weeks on a regular basis to make his closing blessing a reality?

CHAPTER 6: YOUR GOD IS TOO BIG

1. The author claims, "Judaism, Christianity, and Islam...have been journeying in search of the Holy Grail of religious supremacy.... But this quest for greatness has left us with unfulfilled believers and an unimpressed world" (p. 169). To repeat his question at the start of the chapter, in your opinion, "Why do we obsess about a 'great' God and a 'great' religion?" (p. 153).

2. "But what if smallness is divine?" (p. 154), the author asks. "What if our God is too big?" (p. 155). How is the author using the concepts of *bigness* and *smallness*, and how would you answer his questions?

3. Consider how you might have answered Jason: "Why don't religious folk present their ideas where everyone else does? They don't come to book clubs, poetry readings, discussion groups, community service events, and social clubs. There are venues that we as a society set up together for people to share ideas. Why are Christians, and other religious people for that matter, absent from the places where they can't be in charge?" (p. 159).

4. During a radio interview after 9/11, the author observed, "New York is a great opportunity for us Christians to learn. Most of the people here feel that to see the world our way

would be a step backward, morally. They see Christians as people not dedicated to following Jesus on earth, but obsessed with their religion. They see us as people who are not really interested in the sufferings on earth like Jesus was but driven with the need to increase the number of those worshiping this Grand Jesus in heaven. They wonder why, of all people, we are the first to rush to solve the world's problems with weapons instead of patience and humility. I learned that it is we who need to be converted after September 11 to the ways of Jesus" (p. 160). Why do you think that it is so hard for religious people to acknowledge the gap between their ideals and their practice?

5. An old Macedonian man washed the author's feet the first time and remarked, "This is how God gets things done. This is how God changes the world. This is God's way" (pp. 163–164). The author agrees: "Today, any real changes in the world happen this way, through the unstoppable power of humility.... Our hate does not confuse and disarm the enemy; our love does.... The problem is that we have come to believe that humility doesn't work. Showing weakness is considered naïve" (pp. 164–165). Do you consider this naïve? How might you envision adopting this approach to change?

CHAPTER 7: THE BLESSING OF ATHEISM

1. Where and when have you experienced with friends, lovers, or family "spirited conversations in which we are in a disagreement" that led to "an empty space between us,

a possibility for the emergence of a truly new idea, an unexpected solution, a way forward" (p. 175)?

2. If you come from a religious perspective, review the ideas listed in the section "Atheism at Its Best" on pages 185–189. Are you willing to acknowledge that atheism at its best could be a blessing to you and your faith community, and if so, how could you communicate that to your cobelievers?

3. If you come from the perspective of atheism, review the "At Camera Three" checklist of advice presented on pages 194–195. Are you willing to take these steps in order to be a blessing to religious folks, and if so, how might you take them?

4. "What matters here is that we acknowledge both the good and the bad, the light and the shadow, in the other and seek a way of being together in this world" (p. 196). The "value of the other" is a theme repeated throughout the book and applied to atheists in this chapter. Beyond the categories of atheism and religion, what *others* present you with the greatest challenge of acknowledging their goodness and their light?

5. The author proposes three imaginative questions to ask ourselves and each other (p. 198): "What do you believe in when you believe—or not believe—in God?" "What can you do to seek out, protect, and hear those who subvert your ideas about the God you believe in or don't believe in?" "How can we turn the tensions between us into something life-giving rather than destructive?" Try answering and discussing one of them.

CHAPTER 8: ONE WORLD AT A TIME

1. The little Macedonian church presented the author with a paradox: "In every way I had learned to measure life, these people were just not making it. But there was something at work in and around them that mattered more than anything else I had experienced. What was it?" (p. 205). When and where have you witnessed a similar phenomenon, and what did you conclude accounted for it?

2. The author summarizes the single incentive Jesus offered his followers with the words, "Follow me, and . . . you will learn to love well" (p. 210). In your opinion, was this "woven into all he said and did" (p. 209), and does "You will learn to love well" adequately summarize what Jesus promised his followers?

3. This chapter distinguishes *maps* from *paths* and asserts, "To explain our human experience, discover the meaning of it all, and set goals, we have been looking for the right map, comparing our maps, and arguing about which map is correct" (p. 211). He points out, "The assumption guiding this approach is that life is mostly chaos and has to be reined in. People need to be organized out of 'life as it is' and into the practices and purposes of our religious organizations. . . . Paths are made by walking, and when we get lost in maps, we stop walking" (pp. 211–212). How have you seen this illustrated in the relationships and organizations with which you have been associated?

4. The author portrays Christianity's dichotomy between this world and the next as a misunderstanding of the "good news." "Understood in a lopsided way, 'good news' came to mean the news that believers could go to some other place someday.... The earth is a waiting room; real life is to be found elsewhere and later" (p. 215). How have you seen this emphasis on the afterlife expressed in your religious experience, and what have been the consequences?

5. The author surmises that because "life is the calling," he wanted to "learn to live one world at a time" (pp. 218–219). He emphasizes that "the pearl is... to learn to love well. And the school of that love is life—our ordinary life, the one we have, not the one we wish we had" (p. 220). What could you do to cherish that pearl in the life you have presently?

CHAPTER 9: WHEN MY GOD BECOMES OUR GOD

1. The author argues, "Whatever our beliefs about origins— whether God created us or whether we all came by chance out of some primordial soup—we all come from the same place and are therefore all siblings. Our common origin precedes and therefore supersedes all other identities" (p. 229). When have you seen the interconnectedness of humanity expressed most clearly?

2. If humanity is intricately interconnected, then "our individual dreams are inextricably connected with the lives of other

people, starting with our own family members and extending all the way to people at the other end of the world.... 'It is all about me' plus 'it is all about all of us'" (pp. 230–231). In what ways are your dreams connected to those closest to you and those furthest away?

3. The author asks, "Can Judaism, Christianity, and Islam each be renewed to let God be the God of all humanity?" and answers, "If each can turn to its own history, texts, and traditions and dig deeper than ever before into this theme, change can come" (p. 233). Do you think change is possible? If so, what do you imagine it would take? If not, why not?

4. Commenting on our increasing exposure to other peoples and cultures, the author affirms, "We are stuck together here on this shrinking planet, whether we like it or not, and this reality dawns on us every time we...venture out onto our streets. There are more and more of *the other* in our midst" (p. 243). When and where on a regular basis are you reminded of the prevalence of "*the other* in our midst"?

5. The author contends that the human orientation of wanting to give "keeps us in control, subtly communicating the superiority of our worldview" (p. 241). Therefore, it is more important, especially in matters of God, goodness, and grace, to learn how to receive from others. This is a process that will require time, but how might you initiate the process of receiving from others?

EPILOGUE: MY STORY AND MAYBE YOURS

1. Having followed the author's life throughout the book, how were you affected by the story of his reconciliation with his family on pages 251–257?

2. The author contends, "Understanding our relationship and life with the Divine Other—the Holy One who will always confound us—is inextricably intertwined with our relationship and life with the human other—humanity that also confounds us. The human other is a fractal or a trace of the Divine Other in whose image the stranger has been made" (p. 260). What are similarities between ways in which you have responded to the Divine Other and the stranger?

3. The author claims that the meaning of sacred religious texts such as the Mishnah, the Hebrew Scriptures, the New Testament, and the Quran "will change if they are read *in the presence* of the other" because "when God visits us through *the other*, we are awakened and begin to feel what we could not feel before, we see what we could not see before, and we think what we could not think before. In the presence of *the other*, everything changes" (pp. 260–261). Test this out for yourself. Choose a portion of your sacred text and a person with whom you can sit and read it aloud as if reading for both of you. Then ask the person to share what she has heard from the text and what it means to her. What effect did the presence of the other person have on the meaning you discerned from the text?

4. The author maintains, "We must have a conversation about religion. A broad, deep, and long conversation.... The solutions we cannot find and the blessings we cannot receive are out of our reach precisely because they are where we 'know' they are not!" (pp. 257–258). Make a short list of types of people that, in the past, you have *known* could not be a blessing to you or provide any solutions for you. Having read this book, with whom might you now be willing to risk a "broad, deep, and long conversation"?

5. The author concludes, "To have faith is to set one's heart on and forge a working relationship with a mystery. This can be done in a way that embraces the other or in a way that abandons the other. Our diverse mysteries will remain, but the way we hold them can change. We can hold our mysteries with more laughter about ourselves, more tears for the stranger, and more whirlwind for us all" (p. 270). What steps might you take that would help you "embrace the other" and "hold our mysteries with more laughter" and "more tears for the stranger"?

Ted Ewing, Ph.D., has served as a pastor, professor, and author with an expertise in curriculum development, speaker training, and discussion group leadership training. Ted and Samir became friends during their doctoral programs in religious education (tedewing@gmail.com).

NOTES

Introduction

1. Paul Knitter, "My God Is Bigger Than Your God," *Studies in Interreligous Dialogue*, 2007, *17*(1), 109–110.

2. Samir Selmanovic, "The Sweet Problem of Inclusiveness: Finding Our God in the Other," in Doug Pagitt and Tony Jones (eds.), *An Emergent Manifesto of Hope* (Grand Rapids, Mich.: Baker, 2007); Samir Selmanovic, "Just Religion: Why Should We De-Colonize God's Name?" in Brian McLaren, Elisa Padilla, and Ashley Bunting Seeber (eds.), *The Justice Project* (Grand Rapids, Mich.: Baker, 2009).

Prologue: Life Wins

1. Jalaluddin Rumi, untitled poem (Coleman Barks, trans.), in James Fadiman and Robert Frager, *Essential Sufism* (New York: HarperCollins, 1999), p. 116. This translation first appeared in *Like This: Rumi, 43 Odes, Versions by Coleman Barks* (Athens, Ga.: Maypop Books, 1990), p. 18. Reprinted by permission of Coleman Barks.

2. A common objection to my line of reasoning here would be that the blessing of Israel, known as Abraham's blessing, was not exclusive but instrumental. According to this view, God blessed Israel to be a blessing to all nations (Genesis 12:3, Exodus 19:4–6). The same can be applied to Christians and Muslims. I held this argument in my heart for decades before I came to believe that nations of the world deserve the dignity to be more than objects of our best efforts. In the Kingdom of God, nobody can be objectified. I write about a different view of Abraham's blessing in Chapter Nine.

3. From a standpoint of being a passionate Christian myself, I obviously do believe that the Christian Bible and Jesus are the full revelation of God's nature and will. Similarly, Jews believe this about Torah, and Muslims believe this about Quran and the Prophet Muhammad. I do not hold that these revelations of God are all the same! What Christians mean by "God's grace and unconditional love" is unique, just as, for instance, the Muslim concept of "submitting to no one but God" is unique. The mysteries of our faiths are particular. However, I do believe that they are revelations about the same reality. That reality, for me, is the Kingdom of God that Jesus has talked about. We are all talking about the same life, the same humanity, and the same world. Therefore, although our mysteries differ, God is fully with "them," as God is fully with "us." And this applies to all people groups on the earth, not just Abrahamic religions. Nobody is abandoned.

4. I thank Eboo Patel for helping us name what is wrong with "interfaithing" and see a way forward through spiritual diversity and social action. You can read about his experience in "Real Life Activism," ch. 4 of his book *Acts of Faith: The Story of an American Muslim, the Struggle for the Soul of a Generation* (Boston: Beacon Press, 2007).

5. Parker J. Palmer, *Let Your Life Speak: Listening for the Voice of Vocation* (San Francisco: Jossey-Bass, 2000), p. 34, italics in original.

6. Rainer Maria Rilke, in Babette Deutsch (trans.), *Poems from the Book of Hours* (New York: New Directions, 1941). Reprinted by permission of New Directions Publishing Corp.

7. Ananda K. Coomaraswamy, in Martin Lings and Clinton Minaar (eds.), *The Underlying Religion: An Introduction to Perennial Philosophy* (Bloomington, Ind.: World Wisdom, 2007), p. 217.

8. Ibid., p. 229.

Chapter 1: Living with a Splinter

1. Ecclesiastes 3:11, TNIV.

2. Abraham Joshua Heschel, *Between God and Man: An Interpretation of Judaism* (Fritz A. Rothschild, ed.) (New York: Free Press, 1959), p. 234.

3. Quran 2:256, in Muhammad Asad, *The Message of the Qur'an* (Bristol, England: Book Foundation, 2003).

4. Yehuda Amichai, "The Place Where We Are Right," in Brad Hirschfield, *You Don't Have to Be Wrong for Me to Be Right: Finding Faith Without Fanaticism* (New York: Harmony Books, 2007), p. ix.

Chapter 2: The Secret of the Ordinary

1. Søren Kierkegaard, *Stages on Life's Way* (Walter Lowrie, trans.) (Princeton, N.J.: Princeton University Press, 1945), p. 403.

2. Jalaluddin Rumi, in Daniel Ladinsky (trans.), *Love Poems from God: Twelve Sacred Voices from the East and West* (New York: Penguin Compass, 2002), p. 61. Reprinted by permission of Daniel Ladinsky.

3. Dallas Willard, *The Divine Conspiracy: Rediscovering Our Hidden Life in God* (San Francisco: HarperOne, 1998), p. 14.

4. Vincent J. Donovan, *The Church in the Midst of Creation* (Maryknoll, N.Y.: Orbis Books, 1990), pp. 68–69. Donovan here refers to Karl Rahner, "How to Receive a Sacrament and Mean It," in Michael J. Taylor (ed.), *The Sacraments: Reading Contemporary Sacramental Theology* (New York: Alba House, 1981), p. 74.

5. Palmer, *Let Your Life Speak*, p. 67.

6. Donovan, *Church in the Midst of Creation*, p. 64.

7. Ibid., p. 72.

8. Alexander Schmemann, *For the Life of the World* (Crestwood, N.Y.: Saint Vladimir's Seminary Press, 1973), pp. 75–76. In keeping with English usage at the time the book was written (1963), the author used male nouns and pronouns to stand for all of humanity.

9. John 4:21–24, NIV.

10. Numbers 11:5, NIV.

11. Richard Rohr, "The Great Chain of Being," *Radical Grace*, April–June 2007.

12. Donovan, *Church in the Midst of Creation*, pp. 111, 128.

13. Mark 16:15, NIV.

Chapter 3: God Management Systems

1. Abraham Joshua Heschel, *Between God and Man: An Interpretation of Judaism* (Fritz A. Rothschild, ed.) (New York: Free Press, 1959), pp. 101–102.

2. Amichai, "Place Where We Are Right," p. ix.

3. John 3:8, NIV.

4. Karen Armstrong, *A History of God: The 4,000 Year Quest of Judaism, Christianity, and Islam* (New York: Ballantine Books, 1993), p. 55.

Chapter 4: Why Is God Not More Obvious?

1. Isaiah 55:8, 9, NIV.

2. Isaiah 45:15, NIV.

3. Saint Thomas Aquinas, in Ladinsky, *Love Poems from God*, p. 136. Reprinted by permission of Daniel Ladinsky.

4. Isaiah 55:10, 11(1), NIV.

5. Peter Rollins, *How (Not) to Speak of God* (Brewster, Mass.: Paraclete Press, 2006), p. xii.

6. Isaiah 55:12, NIV.

7. Matthew 11:29, in Eugene H. Peterson (trans.), *The Message: The Bible in Contemporary Language* (Colorado Springs, Colo.: Navpress, 2002), p. 1766.

8. C. S. Lewis, *Surprised by Joy: The Shape of My Early Life* (Boston: Houghton Mifflin, 1995), p. 15.

9. Song of Songs 3:1, 2(1), NIV.

10. Aquinas, in Ladinsky, *Love Poems from God*, p. 138. Reprinted by permission of Daniel Ladinsky.

11. Shams-ud-din Muhammad Hafiz, in Ladinsky, *Love Poems from God*, p. 153. Reprinted by permission of Daniel Ladinsky.

12. Ibid., p. 171. Reprinted by permission of Daniel Ladinsky.

13. Tukaram, in Ladinsky, *Love Poems from God*, p. 349. Reprinted by permission of Daniel Ladinsky.

14. Saint Catherine of Siena, in Ladinsky, *Love Poems from God*, p. 186. Reprinted by permission of Daniel Ladinsky.

15. Saint Theresa of Avila, in Ladinsky, *Love Poems from God*, p. 295. Reprinted by permission of Daniel Ladinsky.

16. Thoughts in this paragraph are taken from Paul Knitter, "My God Is Bigger Than Your God." For this, he credits Ernst Troeltsch, *The Absoluteness of Christianity*

(Richmond: John Knox, 1971) and Krister Stendahl, "Notes for Three Biblical Studies," in Gerald Anderson and Thomas Stransky (eds.), *Christ's Lordship and Religious Pluralism* (Maryknoll, N.Y.: Orbis Books, 1981), pp. 7–18.

17. I am thankful to Stephen Hirtenstein, one of the foremost scholars of Ibn 'Arabî, whom I heard at the Open Center in New York City in 2008 sharing Ibn 'Arabî's concept of the Brotherhood of Milk. An extensive paper titled "The Brotherhood of Milk: Perspectives of Knowledge in the Adamic Clay" can be found at http://www.ibnarabisociety.org/articles/brotherhood.html.

18. 1 John 4:7–9, 16(2), NIV.

19. Rollins, *How (Not) to Speak of God*, p. 17.

20. Mira, in Ladinsky, *Love Poems from God*, p. 246. Reprinted by permission of Daniel Ladinsky.

Chapter 5: Where Does Your Heart Go?

1. J. Richard Middleton and Brian J. Walsh, *Truth Is Stranger Than It Used to Be: Biblical Faith in a Postmodern Age* (Downers Grove, Ill.: InterVarsity Press, 1995), p. 59.

2. I am deeply thankful to Timothy Keller, theologian and pastor of Redeemer Presbyterian Church in New York City, for teaching me about this biblical concept of idolatry from an evangelical perspective.

3. Psalm 63:1, NIV.

4. Psalm 63:3, NIV.

Chapter 6: Your God Is Too Big

1. Milan Kundera, *The Unbearable Lightness of Being: A Novel* (New York: Harper-Perennial, 2008). (Originally published 1984.)

2. Mark 4:30–31, NIV.

3. In *Your God Is Too Small* (New York: Touchstone, 2004), first published in 1952, J. B. Phillips argued for breaking through our static discussions about God and conceiving of God as big enough to command our highest admiration and respect. My discussion here is not an attempt to contradict, much less refute this notion. I merely argue that using the adjective "great" to describe God has its own limitations.

4. John 13:1–17, NIV.

5. See Isaiah 58, NIV.

6. 1 Kings 19:11–13(1), NIV.

7. Hebrews 4:12, NIV.

8. John 12:24, NIV.

Chapter 7: The Blessing of Atheism

1. Lee Siegel, "Militant Atheists Are Wrong," *Los Angeles Times*, Oct. 7, 2007.

2. Acts 1:8.

3. Armstrong, *History of God*, p. xxi.

4. Ibn 'Arabî, *Futuhat al-Makkiyya*, Vol. 4 (Beirut, Lebanon: Dar Sadr, n.d.), pp. 420, 386.

5. Rollins, *How (Not) to Speak of God*, p. 27.

6. Andrew Sullivan, "When Not Seeing Is Believing," *Time*, Oct. 9, 2006.

7. Merold Westphal, *Suspicion and Faith: The Religious Use of Modern Atheism* (New York: Fordham University Press, 1998).

8. Ross Douthat, "Probably and Perhaps," *Atlantic*, Jan. 16, 2009, http://rossdouthat.theatlantic.com/archives/2009/01/probably_and_perhaps.php.

9. I am not talking here about humanism or other worldviews that find their identity in something more than merely rejecting the notion of the existence of God. I am talking here about atheism in the narrow sense of the word and about the ways it can serve the world made of both theists and atheists. My use of the phrase "atheism at its best" is in the context of *makhloket* and in the spirit of seeking for the way atheists can be a blessing to their opponents.

10. John D. Caputo, *What Would Jesus Deconstruct: The Good News of Post-Modernism for the Church* (Grand Rapids, Mich.: Baker Academic, 2007).

11. André Glucksmann, *Dostoïevskià Manhattan* [*Dostoyevsky in Manhattan*] (Paris: Laffont, 2002). I owe insights from this and the following paragraph to the Slovenian philosopher Slavoj Žižek, particularly his chapter "Anonymous Religion of Atheism" in *Violence: Six Sideways Reflections* (New York: Picador, 2008).

12. Sigmund Freud, *The Future of an Illusion* (New York: Norton, 1989). (Originally published 1927.)

13. Sigmund Freud, *Moses and Monotheism* (London: Vintage, 1955). (Originally published 1939.)

14. For a short overview of Freud's relationship with religious beliefs, see Mark Edmundson, "Defender of Faith?" *New York Times Magazine*, Sept. 9, 2007.

15. William B. Parsons, *The Enigma of the Oceanic Feeling: Revisioning the Psychoanalytic Theory of Mysticism* (Oxford: Oxford University Press, 1999), p. 45. I thank Nancy Fuchs-Kreimer from Reconstructionist Rabbinical College in Pennsylvania for helping me with this reference.

16. Gregory Epstein, *Good Without God: What a Billion Nonreligious People Do Believe* (New York: Morrow, 2009).

17. David Niose, "Harvard Humanism: Beyond the Walls of Secular Cathedral—The *Humanist* Interview with Gregory Epstein," *Humanist*, Mar.–Apr. 2007, p. 20.

Chapter 8: One World at a Time

1. Luke 3:21. See also Matthew 3:13–17, NIV.

2. Matthew 16:24, NIV.

3. Willard, *Divine Conspiracy*, p. 302.

4. I heard this story as a student at Andrews University Theological Seminary in the early 1990s, from Professor Jacques Doukhan in the class Jewish Life and Thought.

5. See Matthew 16:21–23, NIV.

6. Acts 15:13–15, NIV.

7. Ante said he was paraphrasing George Hunsinger's comment on Karl Barth's *Church Dogmatics* in *How to Read Karl Barth: The Shape of His Theology* (Oxford: Oxford University Press, 1993), pp. 27–28.

Chapter 9: When My God Becomes Our God

1. Miroslav Volf, *Exclusion and Embrace: A Theological Exploration of Identity, Otherness, and Reconciliation* (Nashville, Tenn.: Abingdon Press, 1996), pp. 63–65.

2. Miroslav Volf, "Living with the Other," *Ministry*, Mar. 2007, p. 7.

3. Volf, *Exclusion and Embrace*, chs. 1–4.

4. C. S. Lewis, *The Weight of Glory* (San Francisco: HarperOne, 2001), p. 154.

5. Genesis 12:1–3, NIV.

6. Quoted by Erick J. Schelske in "Is There No Privacy?" *Touchstone*, July–Aug. 2001, p. 13.

7. Kuan Tao-Sheng, untitled poem, in Theodor Reik, *Of Love and Lust* (New York: Farrar, Straus & Giroux, 1949), p. 73.

8. Admittedly, each of these three religions have texts calling for violence (apparently coming from God). I believe these forceful calls were given primarily to assist people who were reluctant to take necessary steps to ensure their survival. For the texts that do not allow for interpretation of violence as self-defense, I believe it would be better to modify our views of revelation and inspiration. We should interpret these individual texts in light of a comprehensive message of the entire text (justice, peace, beauty, and so on) rather than cling to—or should I say idolize—our preferred and often static views of revelation and inspiration. Such principles not only condone violence—which is a reason enough to ditch them—but also create violence. There are additional comments about the issue of our texts in the Epilogue.

Epilogue: My Story and Maybe Yours

1. John 14:6, NIV.

2. Leviticus 19:33, 34, NIV.

3. Matthew 25:31–46, NIV.

4. Hirschfield, *You Don't Have to Be Wrong*.

5. This "ethics of the other" has been developed by continental philosopher Emmanuel Levinas.

6. Charter for Compassion, http://www.charterforcompassion.com.

7. Karen Armstrong, *The Bible: A Biography* (New York: Atlantic Monthly Press, 2007), pp. 228–229.

8. Jonathan Sacks, *The Dignity of Difference: How to Avoid the Clash of Civilizations* (New York: Continuum, 2003), p. 8.

9. Sacks, *The Dignity of Difference*, p. 19.

10. Paul Knitter, *Introducing Theologies of Religion* (Maryknoll, N.Y.: Orbis Books, 2002), p. 142.

11. G. K. Chesterton, *Orthodoxy* (San Francisco: Ignatius Press, 1995). (Originally published 1908.)

12. Willard, *Divine Conspiracy*, p. 238.

13. Thomas Oden, *The Living God: Systematic Theology*, Vol. 1 (San Francisco: HarperOne, 1992), pp. 405–406.

14. Thomas Merton, *Conjectures of a Guilty Bystander* (New York: Doubleday, 1966), pp. 66–67.

THE AUTHOR

Samir Selmanovic, Ph.d., is an author, speaker, consultant, and community organizer. He was born and raised in a culturally Muslim family in the atheistic urban milieu of Zagreb, the capital of Croatia, in the former Yugoslavia. During his compulsory service in the army, Selmanovic joined an underground group of believers and became a Christian. Upon returning home and announcing his conversion, his family expelled him, sending him off on a long personal journey geographically, culturally, and spiritually.

Selmanovic completed a bachelor of science degree in structural engineering at the University of Zagreb and earned three graduate degrees from Andrews University in Michigan, including a doctorate in religious education. He then served as a pastor and community organizer in Manhattan for six years, which included dealing with the aftermath of the terrorist attacks of September 11, 2001. In 2003, he transferred to Southern California and helped launch and grow CrossWalk Church (http://www.crosswalkvillage.com). In 2008, drawn by his love for New York, he founded and became the Christian coleader of Faith House Manhattan (http://www.faithhousemanhattan.org), an interfaith "community of communities" that brings together forward-looking Christians, Muslims, Jews, atheists, and others who seek to think interdependently.

Selmanovic is an ordained pastor of the Seventh-day Adventist church and cofounder of Re-church Network (http://www.re-church.org). He has been integral to the birth of the emerging church movement, serving as a member of the Coordinating Group of Emergent Village and representing emergents at the Interfaith Relations Commission of the National Council of Churches (http://www.ncccusa.org/interfaith). He has published articles and book chapters about the interplay of spirituality, religion, Scripture, culture, and leadership. He speaks nationally and internationally on topics of interdependence, religious identity, spiritual practice, leadership, interreligious dialogue, and social justice. He lives in Manhattan with his wife, Vesna, and two daughters, Ena and Leta. They are enthusiastic members of City-lights, a Christian community in Manhattan, "learning to love well" (http://www.citylightscommunity.org).

For events, resources, and other information about the author, go to http://www.samirselmanovic.com.

INDEX